THE
UNITED STATES
AND EUROPE

RIVALS AND PARTNERS

THE
UNITED STATES
AND EUROPE

RIVALS AND PARTNERS

MAX SILBERSCHMIDT

with 107 illustrations, 14 in color

HARCOURT BRACE JOVANOVICH, INC.

To Fritz Wehrli, lifelong friend

1 *Frontispiece*
The Statue of Liberty, since 1886 the familiar beacon on the threshold of the New World, stands here under construction in its Paris workshop. The sculpture of Frédéric Bartholdi, a gift of the French people in the first months of the Third Republic, celebrates, as its title suggests, *Liberty Enlightening the World.*

Translated from the German by J. Maxwell Brownjohn
Picture research: Alla Weaver

© 1972 THAMES AND HUDSON LTD, LONDON

First American edition 1972

ISBN 0–15–105550–5 hardbound
ISBN 0–15–593020–6 paperbound

Library of Congress Catalog Card Number: 78-157879

Printed and bound in Great Britain by Jarrold & Sons Ltd, Norwich

CONTENTS

Throughout this book I have used the word 'billion' in the American sense of a thousand
6 million.

Much has been written on America by Europeans, and Europe has been the subject of numerous studies by Americans. The present study encompasses both Europe and the United States and its object is to inquire how they have influenced, repelled and attracted one another. It is not, however, an attempt at an 'Atlantic history'. The problem of the Atlantic community has occupied a generation of historians, and was thoroughly discussed at the International Conference of Historical Sciences held at Rome in 1955. R. R. Palmer, the American historian, has provided a pioneer study in *The Age of the Democratic Revolution,* as has Jacques Godechot, a Frenchman, in his *Histoire de l'Atlantique.*

I want to adopt a different approach, and to try and sketch the relations between the USA and Europe in the wider context of world history. Only when we place Europe and the United States in a universal context can we perceive how far their histories belong together and how far they have, necessarily, gone their separate ways. We cannot understand what they have meant to one another unless we inquire at the same time what they have meant to the world. Europe and America never directly confronted each other; their encounters always took place in the framework of 'wider associations'. This is why it seems so fascinating to see, as a result of the divergent task or mission which each has assumed or assigned to the other, how they have come closer together, and how each has taken an increasingly intensive interest in its transatlantic partner.

The subject is of fundamental importance and wide in scope. It is also sensitive and involves so many different levels of contact that one might well despair of tackling it successfully. Eminent men have reflected on Europe and America from opposite sides of the Atlantic, but there is a difference between a European – Alexis de Tocqueville, for instance – speaking about America, and Henry Adams speaking about Europe, because their viewpoint and assumptions are not the same. When a Frenchman reflects on Italy and a German on France, and vice versa, their deliberations have a common historical basis. 7

Europeans and Americans have yet to acquire a common history in the narrower sense. Perhaps we may be starting to acquire one, and one central purpose of this study is to discover how much common history we do possess.

That America grew out of Europe, that it was discovered and founded by Europe, that it was a product of the European system of economy and government – all these are important factors. We must never forget that, by reason of its origins, America is part of Europe.

From the very beginning America has been a magnet. It has been a challenge, as if proclaiming: Come and see for yourself what I am! Europeans turned their backs on Europe and emigrated there by the million, and relatively few of those who did so ever returned. A spiritual relationship of a peculiar kind exists between emigrants and those who remain, a relationship always strongly tinged with emotion. The societies set up by the former are seen by those left behind as daughter-states, as communities of European origin, as 'ours' and yet no longer 'ours' – as apostates – because, in their eyes, Europe· (or Eurasia, if one will) remains the homeland and, somehow, the fountainhead of all culture. To the emigrant or newcomer in the lands across the ocean, the picture looks different – perhaps entirely reversed. For them, America is the new Canaan, the true home which has at last been reached, the new man's allotted goal. And yet, even to the immigrants themselves, the new home may mean very different things, depending on their country of origin, on whether they settled in virgin land or in territory that had already been opened up. Descent from the founding fathers became a status symbol and betokened social distinction. By contrast, late arrival became a psychological spur to self-assertion and personal achievement.

The transformation of America took place at a truly breathtaking pace. It has aptly been said that the United States underwent, within a century, a process of development which it took Europe two thousand years to complete, though only the importation of two millennia of experience from Europe made this possible. For its part, Europe is changing and transforming itself faster than ever before, because America relieved the old continent of strain and served as a model or example to spur Europeans on.

Europe and America have always been in a state of mutual tension. They have always regarded one another as different, and designedly so. Hence the permanent dialogue, the everlasting discussion – indeed, the constant debate – between them, analogous to the dialogue between a father and an increasingly adult son.

Fundamentally, the great migration, the exodus from Europe to America, is the central theme of the story. It is not only statistically measurable but also amply documented, even in its spiritual and psychological import. It has now reached something of a standstill and, as a matter of fact, has long been marked, in the economic sphere, by a reverse process, by a return of American business and American capital to Europe.

If there is 'tension' between America and Europe it is because Europeans have never mentally assimilated the fact of America, just as Americans have failed to absorb the fact of Europe. Americans are searching for their identity, just as Europeans, their traditions shaken by America, are searching for their own. Indeed, we are both searching for our identity by fashioning ourselves an anti-world out of the other world. We are engaged in a reciprocal quest in order to manufacture our own image from its counterpart. All serious European literature on the United States is in some way a criticism of Europe – a search for pointers to Europe's future. This applies even to so spiteful and biased a book as Georges Duhamel's *Scènes de la vie future* (1930).

The United States is in such a lively confrontation with itself that, ever since it sent its troops to fight on European soil in World War I, some of its greatest writers have emulated Henry James by moving to Europe and – like T. S. Eliot – becoming Europeans themselves. Characteristically it was from across the Atlantic that the cry 'Let there be Europe!' resounded after World War II. The time has indeed come to ask how things stand between Europe and the United States, what 'Europe' and 'America' have to tell one another, and how they will fare together in time to come. In the situation which prevails today it may be that Lewis Mumford's dictum, 'The settlement of America had its origins in the unsettlement of Europe', should be replaced by the suggestion that the unsettlement of America may conduce to a settlement in Europe; or, more significantly and probably, that only the settlement of both America and Europe can offer us all the promise of a brighter future.

9

I AMERICA, THE EUROPEAN DREAM

The discovery of America was the discovery of a dreamed-of world. Plato's Atlantis, legendary Thule and the myth of a paradise on earth were all firmly rooted in the western mind. Now this vision had become reality. To the Pilgrim Fathers, America was the Promised Land. The new Americans, who regarded their annexation of territory and the opening up of an entire continent from the Atlantic to the Pacific as a rebirth of the Old World in new surroundings beyond the seas, wanted to be a living example to the rest of the world.

Europe, which felt the acquisition of America to be an accretion of its own power and wealth, wished to keep the development of its overseas venture under constant supervision – to control, dominate and assimilate it. But in America the spirit of revolt, opposition and resistance awoke. It welled up from the deep-rooted European sense of liberty which had found sanctuary on the other side of the Atlantic, was transfigured by the same belief in America as the Promised Land, and developed into a will to throw off the European yoke.

The defection of the North American colonies, which spread to Central and South America and ultimately embraced the entire double-continent, ushered in the modern era. It provided a beacon for the political and economic revolution which has characterized the last two centuries. Because it started in new colonial territory and then reacted on the Old World, the revolution provoked conflicts which eventually affected the Third World, for the New World felt more of an obligation towards embryonic nations outside Europe than it did towards the older nations from which it was descended.

The discovery of America stemmed from the plan for a maritime link with Asia, which was based on two separate projects: the eastern route favoured by the Portuguese, the western by the Spaniards. The latter came up against the obstacle known as 'America', which Magellan circumnavigated via the southern tip of the continent, thus

2 Christopher Columbus reaches America; symbolic engraving by Théodore de Bry, 1594.

3, 4 The North American Indian:
two European views. Above,
Indian Conjuror by John White, one
of the first colonists of Virginia;
right, Jan Mostaert's fanciful
representation of the conquest of
the new continent.

leading to the discovery of the Pacific islands and, later, of Australia,
New Zealand and Antarctica. The establishment of plantations in the
tropical and subtropical coastal regions of America and in the island
possessions of the Caribbean was made possible only by the exploitation
of a human reservoir of African slaves. Trade with these plantations
attained substantial dimensions and became important enough to
cause a series of colonial wars among the European maritime powers.
The same applied to the trade in beaver skins, pursued in association
with the North American Indian tribes of the St Lawrence basin,
where French, English and Dutch interests came into conflict. The
French, who were most successful of all at borrowing from the Indians
and assimilating Indian modes of life, pushed furthest into the North

American continent and reached the Rocky Mountains. Meanwhile, the Russians, proceeding from Asia in an easterly direction, and following the route taken in prehistoric times by America's earliest settlers, reached the American continent from eastern Siberia and Alaska. Spaniards, British and Russians developed a brisk trade on the Pacific coast of America, where commercial links between Mexico, the Philippines and China had already been fostered at an earlier date.

The Atlantic region of North America became strategically important during the eighteenth century as a consequence of the major wars fought for the domination of Indian and American trade (the War of the Spanish Succession and the Seven Years' War). Prominent Europeans focused their attention on America, and Americans

5 *Penn's Treaty with the Indians*, Edward Hicks's celebrated painting, *c.* 1840, shows the ideal of colonist-Indian relations.

maintained close contact with Europe as exponents of the new spirit of enlightenment. The American War of Independence, or (as the insurgents called it) the American Revolution, was rooted in an appeal to the conscience of Europe (the Declaration of Independence, 1776).

What was the basis of this appeal? Its roots reach back into the previous century. For example, Cotton Mather, the seventeenth-century author of *Magnalia Christi Americana*, wrote that his purpose was to 'describe the wonders of the Christian religion, having fled from the iniquities of Europe to the shores of America'. Jonathan Edwards, one of the leading Protestant theologians of the eighteenth century, declared that 'the Old World slew Christ', but that the New World, although equally beset by sin and victorious only by reason of the dialectic of history, was – if such a hope still existed – 'the hope of the world'. Also worth recalling is the poem 'America or the Muse's Refuge' – dedicated to the Americans by Bishop Berkeley, the philosopher, who later travelled to Rhode Island to convert the

Indians to Christianity – with its celebrated line, 'Westward the course of Empire takes its way . . .'.

In these and other similar texts we can already perceive the emergence of the new intellectual movement, a movement which saw America as the arena where a more enlightened and therefore better order of society would be established. The same thought was expressed by John Trumbull, the celebrated 'Hartford Wit', whose 'A Prospect of the Future Glory of America' (1770) boldly proclaimed that America would see 'some Shakespeare charm the rising age'.

Contact with non-European civilizations transformed the European view of man and the world during the age of enlightenment. If, at first, the Red Indian was admired as an unspoiled child of nature, those who concurred in Voltaire's description of happiness as a product of civilization later transferred their admiration to the American settlers. 'The myth of the "noble savage" served as a basis for admiration of the free white man who enjoys his natural rights and is conscious of his human dignity.' The Frenchman Guillard de Beaurieu declared, 'Americans, with you there are no large towns, no luxury, no crimes and no diseases. You are as Nature commands us all to be.' One is reminded of John Locke's remark (in his *Second Treatise of Government*), 'In the beginning all the world was America!'

America at this time felt itself intimately linked with Europe, as befitted a progressive province of the west. The best of its sons were sent to Europe to be educated at centres of learning there. Then, thanks to a strange concatenation of events, the British colonies became embroiled in a legal and economic tussle with the motherland which led, by way of war and revolution, to the founding of the United States and the beginning of a new chapter in world history.

The conflict which led to the Declaration of Independence in 1776 was concluded by the Peace of Paris in 1783. The constitution of 1787 and the installation as President of the former revolutionary general, George Washington, demonstrated that, for the first time, an independent country had been founded on the other side of the Atlantic. The new development had a profound effect on Europe. It delighted all European devotees of liberty and provoked a surge of love and affection for America. Interest in America was overshadowed for a time by the outbreak of the French Revolution, which, though not directly set in motion by the American example, was clearly inspired by it. In the end, however, when Napoleon became 15 the heir of the revolution, plunged Europe into war and brought it under his personal dominion, the achievements of the Americans shone even more brightly.

The period between 1775 and 1815 – indeed the whole period until 1823 – is fundamental for any understanding of the relationship between the Old and New Worlds. This was when the course was set, basic standpoints adopted, and even if the relationship was redefined in 1949, the attitude adopted by the Founding Fathers remains a precedent and established criterion still valid for the generation of Americans alive today.

As everyone knows, the American rebels of the 1770s enjoyed the approval of many of their English cousins, who indulged in panegyrics about the American settlers' bold but well-considered venture. No one espoused the Americans' cause more ardently than Edmund Burke; Adam Smith was another who viewed their aims with favour. To such men, the American fight for freedom was a fight for the freedom of Europe. The course of events seemed to confirm this belief, because George III's personal régime collapsed and Britain's internal development was decisively influenced by the work of those politicians – notably William Pitt the Younger – who had advocated a new line during the critical years in question.

By taking a stand against the French Revolution the British moved closer in principle to the newly formed Union, whose value as a factor in power politics was thereby enhanced. The British also adopted, in a modified form, certain political innovations born of the American Revolution and introduced them into their colonial policy (Canada, Ireland), as well as into their commercial policy (abolition of the slave trade, free trade). In relation to party organization and election campaigns, too, America provided a variety of stimuli. Thus, although Britain relinquished its Atlantic colonies (while retaining Canada), the legacy of a common political origin continued to play a part in Anglo-American relations.

By founding a new state, America had earned itself a place outside Europe. Spurred on by the happy circumstance of a major migration westwards, it became – once it had 'detached', indeed, divorced itself from Europe – the land of Manifest Destiny, of the great departure, and of a new continental nationalism. And yet, particularly to those Europeans who remained faithful to the American idea, it remained

the land of hope and of the future. The American myth continued to enjoy the favour of those who were dedicated to the concept of liberty.

It is scarcely possible to speak of an American type prior to Benjamin Franklin, who delighted in roaming Paris as a foreigner and in being admired as an American. And yet one should not forget that Franklin spent sixteen years of his life in England and nine in France, and might well be regarded as a European. 'Franklin betrays neither nostalgia nor alienation,' writes Melvin Lasky, 'those emotions so characteristic of his fellow-countrymen. He considers the unity of civilization and the world-embracing brotherhood of all thinking people to be absolute and natural. The difference between the Old and the New World was in his view not of a moral and cultural but of a political and economic nature.' He was, of course, fond enough of his homeland to suffer gladly the affection which people felt for him as an American – a sentiment so widespread that even Marie Antoinette referred to him as 'notre cher Républicain'. Voltaire insisted on attending the baptism of Franklin's grandchild and blessed it with the words 'God and liberty'. A famous French privateer was christened Bonhomme Richard, and the French battle-song 'Ça ira, ça ira' derived from Franklin's commentary on the American War of Independence.

6 Support for the American cause in an English cartoon of 1775. George III, driven by Pride and Obstinacy, running roughshod over the Constitution and Magna Carta, rushes headlong into disaster, while America burns on the horizon.

7 Benjamin Franklin, writer, printer, scientist, diplomat and republican, predicted as early as 1768 the colonies' eventual demands for independence. Here he appears as a Staffordshire figure of the late eighteenth century.

8 The American delegates to the Peace of Paris in 1783; the sketch (incomplete because the British signatories refused to pose) is by Benjamin West, one of the first American painters to gain international recognition. Benjamin Franklin is the centre figure.

In this world of reformist zeal and quest for enlightenment, it was Europeans who predicted a future in which America would, with incalculable results, detach itself from Europe. This is evident from Robert Turgot's memorandum of 6 April 1776, in which he discusses the attitude to be adopted by France in face of the rising storm in America. Whichever way the battle went, he said, nothing would prevent the colonies from winning absolute independence of England, a fact which would entirely revolutionize relations between America and Europe and usher in a period of political and economic upheaval, not only within the British Empire but throughout the world.

The American Revolution was a product of the European Age of Enlightenment. It was Thomas Paine's polemic, *Common Sense*, that

prodded the Americans – at a time of uncertainty and a search for a way out – towards a republican form of government and estranged them from the British political tradition. Published on 10 January 1776, *Common Sense* invested the Declaration of Independence with persuasive impact. Returning to England, Paine wrote *The Rights of Man* in rebuttal of Burke's *Reflections*, and was then elected to the French National Convention, from which Robespierre later expelled him. But when he returned to his adopted home in America in 1802 the cosmopolitan Paine met with incomprehension. His tragic fate reflects the two phases of the American Revolution, one internationalist, universalist and rationalist in tone, and the other already tinged with conservatism and nationalism in the Burkian mould.

9 John Singleton Copley's portrait of the Americans Mr and Mrs Ralph Izard, 1775, against a background fully in keeping with contemporary European classicism.

To Americans, the founding of the United States appeared to create a structure which they regarded as the antithesis of Europe, yet they themselves were scions of Europe – Europeans by language, law, custom and religion. A problem of identity arose in consequence. Already in the colonial era discussion centred on what an American was. St John de Crèvecœur, the French nobleman who became an American, gave a now classic definition in his *Letters from an American Farmer* (1782). 'They are a mixture of English, Scotch, Irish, French, Dutch, Germans and Swedes. . . . He [the American] is arrived on a new continent; a modern society offers itself to his contemplation, different from what he had hitherto seen. . . . Here are no aristocratical families, no courts, no kings, no bishops, no ecclesiastical dominion, no invisible power giving to a few a very visible one. . . .'

With the founding of the United States, the question of how far people felt they still wished to belong to Europe became a matter of practical importance. On the intellectual plane, in language, law, religion, literature, amenities, consumer goods, trade, science and technology there could be no break, or no immediate wish for separation, because dependence on and attachment to Europe was not only natural but expedient. But the picture changed with the trek to the West and the building of a continental empire so vast that it permitted a large measure of self-sufficiency.

The quest for the intrinsic value of American culture involved a constant problem of self-assertion. At first it was the Europeans who enthusiastically affirmed America's individuality and regarded the American way of life as exemplary; but their attitude yielded to a wave of revulsion which bordered on condemnation. This volte-face was a result not only of the increase in US power-potential but also of changed intellectual attitudes in Europe and America. In Europe, the age of cosmopolitan enlightenment, and the revolutionary and Napoleonic periods, were succeeded by the age of Biedermeier and the Romantics, with its reversion to the past, its revaluation of tradition and history, its doctrine of the 'organic' national state, sustained by a linguistic and ethnic community with deep roots in the past. Seen from this angle, cultural developments in the United States could not but be regarded as retrogressive, American civilization as a rootless, superficial way of life which soon came to be represented 21 as the culture of the dregs of humanity. Later, when European powers competing for world markets and the chance to exploit new colonial territories recognized America to be a serious rival, the reaction in Europe was quite different, and it was different again when the United States – first in 1917 and for a second time in 1944 – set foot on European soil as a military power and was crowned with success in battle.

The American historian, Daniel J. Boorstin, in his study *America and the Image of Europe*, has shown how Americans necessarily made Europe the criterion of their self-awareness, using the idea of a polarity between America and Europe to reach an understanding of themselves.

For Americans, the problem was that they could not abandon their roots without risking an immense cultural loss – something which American writers have only too frequently experienced. On the other hand, the United States aspired to be more than a mere epilogue to European history, more than a 'newer old world'. Hence it is understandable that the idea of America as the antithesis of Europe – another entirely different world – forms a basic thread of the entire debate, and one which has consistently been emphasized for propaganda purposes. From Crèvecœur, via Jefferson and Emerson to Henry Adams, there has always been a perceptible undertone which implies, 'But of course, we are better people.' Boorstin shows how this polarity can be traced right through to the era of the Cold War, when an (anti-American) 'communist world' was contrasted with an (American) 'anti-communist world'. The present generation knows how pernicious such antitheses can become.

Those with more perception realized, however, that merely to contrast Europe and America was not enough, and that America must somehow progress beyond Europe; the more prophetic writers pointed the way. As Halvdan Koht says of Walt Whitman: 'He spoke the voice of prisoners and slaves, of all the oppressed generations and beings. It was the American program of the equal freedom of all men transformed into the triumphal hymn of infinite expansion. And it was the ideal of universal fraternity, the noble comradeship of men and nations. He was America's greatest message to the world.' Boorstin is fully aware of the difficulty of being the capital of the world while still a province of Europe. After the 'lost generation' had sought its home in Europe at the end of World War I, returning to the fountainhead of culture, a new generation of American writers who had also participated in the battle for Europe discovered a distinctive literary language of their own, which was accepted and recognized in Europe. Hemingway, Faulkner, Wilder, Thomas Wolfe and Arthur Miller have become writers of European repute. The common confrontation with the danger of the atom bomb, of totalitarianism and the subordination of man in technological society has brought both parties closer together in Wendell Willkie's concept of the 'One World'.

If it was the slogan of youthful decadence which made the young American republic hope that its mission would be to revive western civilization, today a deep sense of national decadence is prevalent within the United States. The expectation that Europe would be reborn in America is no longer valid, but on the other hand Europe and the United States have become more alike, their destinies more closely interwoven. For Emerson it was still true that when Americans went to Europe, they became more Americanized. Paul Valéry, on the other hand, wrote in 1938 that whenever he despaired of Europe, his only hope was in thinking of the New World. T. S. Eliot saw his only prospect of fulfilment and maturity in becoming a European. The more prophetic of American writers (Melville and Emerson, for instance) knew better; they were inheritors not merely of one culture but of all. With a literature of social revolt (the Muckrakers, Lewis, Dreiser, Steinbeck, Lincoln Steffens) and existentialist questioning, with Negro spirituals and pop-art, and finally with the burgeoning literature of Afro-Americans (Wright, Baldwin, Cleaver), it is America that is confronting the world with the questions which are of crucial importance for the present generation.

THE LURE OF AMERICA

America succeeded in remaining the European dream because, even after its political foundation, it remained a new country. The opening up of the West attracted swarms of people to America, and the country continued to be a sanctuary for immigrants driven there by undiminished persecution and oppression. At the very same time as the American state was drawing apart from Europe, America as the land of unlimited opportunity, was becoming a universal magnet.   23

The United States found its own particular ethical and political stance, a stance which it has preserved throughout the two hundred years of its history. Its coolness towards the French Revolution was of crucial importance. Jacobinism made few friends in America and even failed to gain formal recognition. The US government eventually took sides with Napoleon in the war of 1812–14, this time not as an ally of France but out of a determination not to miss an opportunity of fighting Britain as long as the conquest of Canada seemed feasible. This clearly disclosed a trend towards an independent policy, which will be discussed later.

The drafting of the constitution of the United States, and the attitude of Franklin and Washington, confirmed pro-American Europeans in their enthusiasm for America. The Marquis de Condorcet was moved by the exemplary way in which the Americans had made the transition from words to deeds. Robespierre paid tribute to Benjamin Franklin in his first public address, and Herder characterized him as a new Socrates. Conversely, the American explorer and archaeologist John L. Stephens called the scientist Alexander von Humboldt 'the greatest man since Aristotle'. Christoph Wieland saw the fighters of the Revolutionary War as Plutarchian heroes, and Friedrich Klopstock declined to return the diploma making him an honorary citizen of the French Republic to the Convention because he wished to remain a 'fellow-citizen of Washington'.

America plays a role of fundamental importance in Goethe's writings. He not only lent poetic utterance, in his famous verses dedicated to the United States, to his faith in America's future – 'America, you are more fortunate than our continent . . .' – but he also voiced ideas in *Dichtung und Wahreit, Wilhelm Meister* and the conclusion of *Faust* which implied that, for him, America was a model of civic fortitude and represented a world where man could carve out a worthy existence by diligence and public spirit. Hence his numerous hints at the possibility that he might emigrate to America. There is no doubt which republican constitution Goethe envisaged in the *Ur-Meister* and in *Wilhelm Meisters Lehrjahre*. His model was the republic, just coming into existence, which was then on everyone's lips, namely, the United States of North America. As the *Lehrjahre* unfolds, so the North American Union, struggling for liberation and then liberated, emerges ever more distinctly, not only as an object of ethical comparison or social paradigm but increasingly as the goal

10 Goethe dictating to his secretary in the last years of his life.

towards which his narrative points. Under the impact of France's economic collapse as a result of the traffic in *assignats*, the American Revolution, far more so than the French, became a determining factor in Goethe's mind. On Goethe's advice, Karl August of Weimar purchased dollars in New York and acquired interests in some Mexican silver mines.

Goethe's work on the *Wanderjahre* spanned a period of over twenty years, during which time he did more than gain an increased knowledge of America. The state of Europe had deteriorated in the post-Napoleonic period. Political reaction in Europe reinforced Goethe's confidence in the Union's capacity for development, and his American plans steadily crystallized as the *Wanderjahre* progressed. The conclusion of *Faust II*, with its scheme for colonization and development, was very probably inspired by Goethe's vision of America. At that time, growing industrialization was precisely what impelled the artisan class to cross the Atlantic. 'To a Europe menaced by technology the condition of the craftsman in America appears, by contrast, advantageous', writes Urzidil, pointing out the prominent role which Goethe at this time assigned to handicrafts and manual labour. Also worth noting is Goethe's remark to Eckermann about the necessity of cutting through the isthmus of Panama in order to establish a direct connection between the Atlantic and the Pacific, which shows Goethe recognized the fundamental importance of America's links with the Far East.

What emerges again and again from Goethe's observations about America is his emphasis on the moral aspect. He saw America's religious liberalism as a model of intellectual freedom everywhere. The celebrated remark in Goethe's letter to Schiller (19 December 1798) in which he writes that he abominates 'everything that merely instructs me without augmenting my activity or directly invigorating it', and his comment that he found 'the contemporaneous the most important because it is most purely reflected in us as we are in it' (*Zur Morphologie* 1/4, 1822), are tokens of his inner affinity with the spirit of America.

America also had a magical attraction for Alexis de Tocqueville. To him, America remained a myth, a utopia, a vision of the future. 'I confess', he wrote, 'that in America I saw more than America, I sought the image of democracy itself, with its inclinations, its character, its prejudices, and its passions. In order to learn what we have to

11 Alexis de Tocqueville, one of the most penetrating European commentators on American democracy; drawing by Théodore Chassériau, c. 1835.

fear or to hope from its progress . . . I have turned my thoughts to the Future.' And then Tocqueville continues with his famous analysis of a democratic world ruled by the principle of equality. The picture which emerges, as Golo Mann has observed, is one which, seen from our own day and reduced to fundamentals, might almost have been intended as a foreword to Riesman's *The Lonely Crowd*. The whole problem of authority and freedom is stated. Tocqueville visited the United States during the era of the Jacksonian Common Man, and his ideas were influenced by friends in the anti-Jacksonian camp. Hence the critical, probing and pessimistic undertone which so delighted American intellectuals that Tocqueville's *De la démocratie en Amérique*, like his compatriot André Siegfried's more recent book, *Les États-Unis d'aujourd'hui*, was pronounced obligatory college reading.

Tocqueville kindled a spirit of American self-criticism. Swiftly seized upon by European detractors of America, his book provided welcome material which, after due processing in Europe, was served up to Americans as a native dish. We can undoubtedly sense a pessimistic undertone in Tocqueville, an expression of his fears for the future, but we can also sense his readiness to 'understand'. He saw that the trend towards material prosperity, the focus upon manufactures and trade, was sustained by passionate religiosity. He saw that the despotism of the majority was mitigated by the rule of custom and tradition. Tocqueville knew well how to distinguish between the 'problem of democracy' and the American democracy of his own day. It was America which set limits upon subjection to the collective. Tocqueville conjured up the spectre of mass existence for all in the west to see. To him, as to Goethe, America was the harbinger of a new era. In Tocqueville we are faced with the approach of industrial-democratic society 'in a chemically purer form' (as Hendrik de Man puts it), with the pattern towards which Europe was moving.

All debate about America remains centred on the problems Tocqueville underscored. The sceptics all cling in some way to the 'negative utopia' (Golo Mann) which he expounded, particularly the Romantics, to whom this middle-class world and these staunch fighters for a just existence could signify nothing. No contemporary has vented more spleen on the United States than Knut Hamsun, a genuine descendant of those who were disillusioned by America, of Nikolaus Lenau and August von Platen, Hoffmann von Fallersleben, Heine (in his later years), Friedrich Schlegel and Dickens. Rootless adventurers, products of speculative finance capitalism – such were those whom Goethe still regarded as forgers of their own happiness. Not so Eichendorff, in his poem 'The Emigrant', with its attack on 'Europe, false creature . . .'; he at least still conveys a palpable sense of the common destiny of Europe and America.

America's contribution to cultural and political history was spontaneously acknowledged at the beginning of the nineteenth century by figures of great eminence. A German-American speaking at the Congress of Vienna drew an enthusiastic picture of America which (to Gentz's horror) was received with deep emotion. And Alexander von Humboldt, speaking of the US administration, ventured to tell the King of Prussia, 'Your Majesty, it is a government which no one sees or feels, yet it is far more powerful than Your Majesty's government.'

With the opening up of a vast continent, the spirit of enlightenment and the Puritan tradition between them carved out a place for the bourgeois world of people's dreams.

Thanks to the trek westwards and the rising tide of immigrants from ever more remote countries, the United States underwent a continuous process of transformation and self-regeneration. Detached from Europe, it created a history of its own. The Atlantic East became the motherland, the metropolis which bade or encouraged its sons to go West. In reality they went West in company with the sons and daughters of Europe. In this westward migration, the United States experienced its Romantic phase – one which it has given back to Europe during the twentieth century in the Wild West clichés of Hollywood, with their popular compound.of daring and brutality, savagery and bravado, loyalty and perfidy, sovereign calm and grim fanaticism.

Here, probably, lies the secret of American magnetism. America remained 'the land of the free', and its freedom assumed gigantic and superhuman dimensions. Who did not wish to participate! A thread runs from Emerson to Nietzsche (as he himself admits) and from Nietzsche to National Socialism, and the link is the Western pioneer, whom the National Socialists willingly adopted as a model. Admittedly, the German road ran eastwards and the *Untermensch* was a Slav instead of a Red Indian, but extermination of the enemy was implicit in each process of territorial aggrandizement.

No one can accuse America of vulgarity unless he counts himself *a priori* a member of some élite. The American does not question a newcomer about his past; all that interests him is the present and how he tackles it, successfully or otherwise. Thus throughout the nineteenth century, America remained the land of hope, or rather the republic of hope, the goal of all those stranded in, outlawed by or banished from Europe.

Young Germany and Young Italy were on good terms with Young America. All those who thirsted for a national reawakening looked towards America. The Frenchman La Fayette is the most famous; but his fame should not be allowed to obscure the memory of von Steuben, the Prussian who was a member of Washington's staff. Poland was represented by Kosciusko and Pulaski, and the former, like La Fayette, carried the fight back to his native land. The 'Decembrist' revolution in Russia was supported by aristocrats noted for their pro-Americanism. Russian intellectual revolt, from Herzen to Bakunin and Kropotkin, is inseparable from the example set by the United States. Alexander II demanded that 'the American language' be introduced into Russia's military academy. Francis Lieber and Carl Schurz transferred their struggle for freedom from Germany to America, where they became distinguished public figures. Mazzini and Garibaldi realized that the United States represented 'the only bulwark against despotism in Europe'.

Within the Swiss Confederation, the campaign to create a Bund (1815–48) was attended by much debate about the example set by the creation of the American federation. Many countries adopted from the United States the principle of the separation of church and state, or the American type of bicameral system. The United States embarked on the further democratization of the electoral system and pioneered new forms of electoral organization (bosses, party bureaucracies and conventions), and was followed cautiously by Europe during the latter half of the nineteenth century. For its part, the Swiss Federal State introduced the Americans to instruments of direct democracy – e.g. national petitions and the referendum – which were much imitated at state level or led to even more radical forms of democratic control such as judicial 'recall', which is practised in one or two Western states. The Swiss militia system enjoyed considerable favour in professional military circles in the United States after World War I, but the American experience during the 1930s and

1940s – the transition from extreme neutrality to massive intervention in world politics – promoted the creation of a professional army.

By upholding the ideas of the age of enlightenment the United States secured itself a 'middle position'. While Europe was oscillating between left and right, between conservative reaction and socialist revolution, and while ideological controversies were rending European parliaments and causing frequent changes of government – and, ultimately, changes of régime to which the most illustrious dynasties succumbed – political life in the United States remained based on the two-party system. This was less a reflection of ideological or class conflicts than of variations in regional structure between East, South and West, as well as of antagonism between urban and agricultural interests.

The United States has been reproached for its 'materialism', its concentration on the material things of life, on money and affluence instead of art and the mind. Today, when American writers and artists compete on terms of equality with those of Europe, and New York has become one of the world's major art centres, this stale controversy has lost all sense. Once they had ensured the material foundations of their existence, like earlier generations in Europe, Americans were no slower than Europeans to invest the proceeds of their affluence in works of art or scientific advancement.

It has, of course, long been apparent that money means something different in America than in Europe. Money transforms itself into work (high wages) and goods. It has become a status symbol in itself. The United States squanders its wealth after the manner of European princes and noblemen. In old Europe (particularly in Tsarist Russia), in Asia and in Africa, the status symbol was land and rule over land. The nobleman was a land-owner and the lord of the manor. In America, once territorial annexation and 'Southern supremacy' were over and done with, there came into being that world of industry and commodities which converted land, too, into money and created a mobile society no less 'intellectual' than a society of landowners; the difference is that, as an absentee landlord, the landowner is able to cultivate the things of the mind, whereas the industrialist regards his professional labours as a creative (intellectual) activity. Achievement is seen as the criterion of a man's worth, and, since this is rewarded financially, money becomes the universal yardstick in the social hierarchy. America thus represents a society based on performance. Soviet Russia and China aspire to have the same.

Let us see what became of the American dreamland or utopia in the course of the nineteenth century.

In the nineteenth century, America still strove to translate idea into reality and create a paradise on earth. It was in a state of permanent revolution. The intellectual positions of the early days were never entirely abandoned. The influence of European romanticism led American puritanism and common-sense philosophy to adopt elements of German idealism (transcendentalism); more important, however, was the trend towards an increasingly secularized protestantism, which led to a variety of practical reform movements. These kept American democratic society constantly on the move. Parallel with

12 'George Shelby giving liberty to his slaves': George Cruikshank's illustration to *Uncle Tom's Cabin*, the Harriet Beecher Stowe novel that played such a large part in popularizing the abolitionist cause.

13 Opposite, temperance banner of 1851 proclaims the merits of love, purity and fidelity.

VIRTUE, LOVE & TEMPERANCE.

LOVE, PURITY & FIDELITY.

GRAND, NATIONAL, TEMPERANCE BANNER.

Dedicated to every Son & Daughter of Temperance, throughout the Union.

LITH. & POB. BY N. CURRIER, 152 NASSAU ST. COR. OF SPRUCE N.Y.

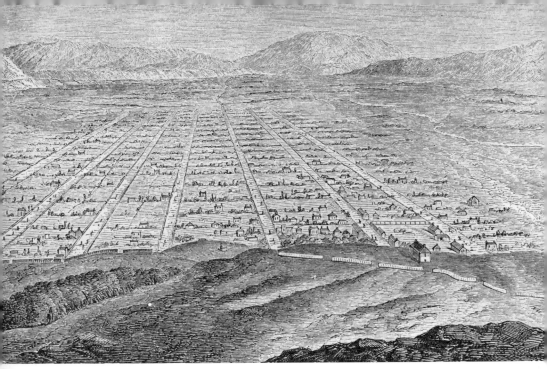

34

14, 15 The Mormons,
members of a religious
movement founded in 1830,
trekked into the unexplored
West and settled in Utah.
Left, Salt Lake City in 1861;
right, Temple Square today.

16 Below, view of the
short-lived Owenite
community at Harmony,
Indiana, in 1825.

35

this we can observe a renewed quest for a still undiscovered Canaan: the Mormon movement, one-third of its members consisting of co-religionists from Europe, founded the tabernacle city of Salt Lake in the Utah desert, and carved a new Canaan out of the wilderness.

The feminist movement started in America; once it had secured its position there, it joined forces with the movement's European advocates to bring about the political, economic and social emancipation of women. The origins of the movement, it is worth noting, can be found among the advocates of the abolition of slavery. Early successes were gained at isolated points in the new western territories, where women were granted the right to vote and a genuine opportunity to exercise it. The temperance and pacifist movements likewise found strong expression in the United States, and had worldwide repercussions. In our own century, the ecumenical movement has met with lively support among the churches of America, just as, in general, the United States is the favourite breeding-ground for new sects and cults (Christian Science, for instance), and has also sought and found links with the religions of Asia.

17, 18 Persecuted religious minorities in Europe traditionally found refuge in the New World. Left, Moravians (United Brethren of Moravia), who were members of an Anabaptist missionary movement founded in the sixteenth century, settled largely in Pennsylvania, and are here shown baptizing Indian converts by immersion. The Shakers, above, who came mainly from Great Britain, established communities in New York State, Pennsylvania and Ohio.

At the beginning of the nineteenth century, the Social Utopians, Owenites, Fourierists and disciples of Etienne Cabet chose the United States as their new home, New England having in the meantime furnished itself with a paradise of its own at Concord. But their settlements (in contrast to those of the Mormons) made no headway and eventually disintegrated because the United States itself was an experimental laboratory and wished to remain so, becoming so successful that American reality triumphed over the dreams of visionaries.

American missionary work in China deserves special mention. Here, armed with religious faith and abundant material resources, the United States felt called upon to fulfil a genuine cultural mission. This consisted, apart from religious conversion, in disseminating western education in schools, hospitals and universities, and in assisting China generally in the role of a fraternal protector.

Americans have been notably successful at performing missionary work among foreigners in their own country. It was a shrewd idea, for instance, to pay the indemnities owed by China for damage inflicted during the Boxer Rebellion (1900) into an account which gave Chinese students access to American universities and enabled them to study in the United States. America's influence in the Far East, which was already apparent to the German orientalist Carl Becker during his trip round the world, can be traced to mature decisions of this kind.

CULTURAL PESSIMISM

At the turn of the nineteenth and twentieth centuries, a group of exceptionally gifted members of the James and Adams families – the brothers Henry and Brooks Adams, and Henry and William James – placed their stamp on the American outlook in a way which is particularly relevant to the present study. The Adams brothers recognized the imminence of developments which would lead to a polarization of power between Russia on the one hand and America on the other. While paying due heed to the rise of Germany, Henry Adams did not believe in a great German future. To him, the key to the future lay in the realization of potential natural resources and in the opportunities and shifts of power to which they would conduce. He was only too correct in his intuitive realization that concentration of mechanical power through the conversion of energy would be the central concern of the twentieth century. Brooks Adams foresaw that the coming configuration of power would transform the United States into a 'military power armed to the teeth'. The Adams brothers were the heralds of America's achievement of full maturity as a civilized power, for it was its enrolment in the great-power system that brought it to full awareness of itself.

It was also Henry Adams who, as a corollary to his reflections on the displacement of the political centre of gravity, first coined the idea of an Atlantic community. Henry James was a brilliant representative of the budding expatriate *avant-garde*, men who believed that the only means of fulfilling themselves as Americans was to submit their work to the most stringent criteria possible: in other words, to gain a foothold in Europe. He 'lived' the Atlantic community by making the American-moulded characters in his cosmopolitan novels live and move and have their being in a European environment – though only because he found that this milieu lent itself peculiarly well to a forceful and sensitive portrayal of the moral dilemma in which human beings are enmeshed.

Both Henry James and the Adams brothers were marked by a pessimism new to America. Representatives of an exalted bourgeoisie and sensitive aristocrats of the mind, they were repelled by the vulgar features of the capitalist society of their day and sought consolation in visions of the future or even in emigration back to Europe. Henry Adams sought consolation in Gothic art and expressed his yearnings for the past in his masterly *Mont Saint Michel and Chartres*. One of his best and most revealing poems is 'A Prayer to the Virgin of Chartres'. He takes his place in some ways besides the Swiss cultural historian, Jacob Burckhardt, who, instead of glorifying the Middle Ages like Henry Adams, singled out the Renaissance as the birth of a new human being. Significantly, it is Americans after World War II who have emphasized Burckhardt's importance in intellectual history.

THE TRIUMPH OF TECHNOLOGY

With William James we come to the member of the Adams and James quartet whose fame far surpasses that of the other three. Like his brother Henry, he was intimately acquainted with European 39 culture as a result of living in Europe. In his *Principles of Psychology*, *The Varieties of Religious Experience*, *Pragmatism* and *A Pluralistic Universe* he gave the world the American version of that intellectual upheaval which found expression in Henri Bergson's *élan vital* in France, Hans Driesch's *Neo-Vitalismus* in Germany, and later in Karl Jaspers' psychological philosophy. It was a great spiritual and intellectual turning-point which marked a break with the philosophical presuppositions of the nineteenth century, and ultimately prepared the American and European worlds for an acceptance of existentialist formulations.

The American version – first in James's works and then in John Dewey's – is characterized by an unusually strong emphasis on the factor of experience, and thus on the harmony between mind and cosmos. In the words of Halvdan Koht, 'Mind became a function of living, never static, always dynamic, and life became an effect of progressive selection.' James reaped the benefits of the half-century of evolutionist thought which had grown up around Herbert Spencer and Social Darwinism, while in his *Varieties of Religious Experience* he sought to integrate the Puritan heritage in an open, pluralistic society.

In Dewey this pragmatism is wholly aligned with the development of the new man who transforms the world by means of his existence. The accent is on proving oneself in life. There is a fundamental contrast here with all those doctrines which view suffering as an essential ingredient of human experience, something magnificently palpable in Dostoevsky. In *The Brothers Karamazov* Dmitri, accused of murder, wonders whether he should flee to Siberia or to the 'Promised Land' (America). Ivan advises him to go to America, there to work the land. Dmitri replies, 'But on the other hand, what about my conscience? I should have run away from suffering. . . . What is America? America is nothing but a vain preoccupation with material gain.'

In America, life is welcomed in the sense of the pioneers, that is to say, it has to be proved in terms of concrete and visible achievement, and it only acquires deeper meaning by being lived in and for the community. The way Americans have aligned the historical and anthropological sciences with sociological inquiry shows clearly the extent to which the pragmatic cast of ideas leads away from an idea of the world that sees the dilemma of good and evil, intellect and instinct, authority and freedom as a tragic entanglement, not only inescapable but bound to set man constantly at odds with himself and

40

19 Benjamin Franklin's famous kite experiment led directly to the invention of the lightning conductor.

society. If the task of the intellect is to facilitate action, the value of thought must be measured by its degree of success in helping things along. If one believes that society develops the values appropriate to it, and that the task of sociology is to assist it in revealing and exposing contemporary values so as to eliminate those which have become a hindrance to development and to discover forms which accord with swiftly changing reality, one is really in perpetual quest of salvation. The idea that a society may be in conflict with itself – the 'tragic situation' – is repudiated.

This is where the affinity between American pragmatism and Marxist doctrine springs to the mind. Marxism, too, aspires to overcome the 'self-alienation' of man by revolutionary upheaval and to find salvation in the classless society. Paradoxically, it might be suggested that the Marxist utopia has found its fulfilment, point by point, in America rather than Russia, and that Russia, step by step, has strayed in the opposite direction.

What is important from the point of view of world economics is that, on this intellectual basis and with this intellectual and spiritual disposition, Americans put their pragmatism to work in practice on a vast scale, not only in production but in labour organization, wage policy, and the organization of trade and capital investment. Raymond Bruckberger, a French Dominican who lived for a considerable time in the United States during the 1950s, goes so far as to assert that the true revolutionaries of our century – those who have really accomplished a revolution – are the Americans. They have created something quite new out of the old entrepreneurial capitalism. The United States is not so much a plutocracy as a place where the principle of production has triumphed. The great innovaters were Henry Ford and Samuel Gompers, both of them true working-class types (André Siegfried regards Ford as a symbolic type and contrasts him with Gandhi, a symbolic type of a wholly different kind). Ford not only created a machine – the automobile – of use to all men, but simultaneously introduced a new method of manufacture (the assembly-line) and a new system of payment. Gompers did not lead the workers to the utopia of the class struggle but endeavoured to make them equal partners in modern industrial society.

A generation later, with David Riesman and *The Lonely Crowd* (1951), we find ourselves face to face with quite a different sort of society: Galbraith's 'affluent society'. Riesman and Galbraith follow

20 The Model 'N' Ford of 1906 (predecessor of the more famous Model 'T') was the first standardized, inexpensive automobile manufactured anywhere in the world.

in the footsteps of Thorstein Veblen, the forceful and individualistic social critic from the Middle West, author of *The Theory of the Leisure Class* (1899), who has given to American economics a kind of Marxian bent. In siding with the engineer against the banker, Veblen took the same line as Bruckberger half a century later and undoubtedly eased the passage for the rise of the technocrats.

43

21, 22 The railroad was probably the single most important factor in shaping the character of the continental United States. Left, Sunday entertainment on the Union Pacific in 1875. Right, a poster of 1869 celebrates the completion of the transcontinental link which united the East and West Coasts

The United States has amazed the world by the technological and scientific momentum it has imparted to its economy, a momentum which brought it world leadership in the mid–twentieth century, which made it the first (with the help of immigrant scientists from Europe) to test and manufacture atomic bombs, and to land astronauts on the moon. What paved the way for such achievements was a long succession of inventors stretching from Eli Whitney, via Samuel Colt and Cyrus McCormick, to Thomas Edison. The United States can thank its educational system for the successful linking of science and industry. The staffing of modern industrial enterprises and government may be undertaken only by societies which produce a constant flow of efficient workers and potential managers. This has been effected in the United States by means of a democratic but, at the upper end of the scale, extremely élitist educational system.

When Woodrow Wilson came to Europe at the end of World War I – the first serving President to make such a visit – he was acclaimed as bringing a new political order which would guarantee peace on earth. To many Europeans, he meant what Washington and Lincoln had meant to earlier generations in the Old World. The utopia of a league of free nations fascinated people in the same way as Lenin's gospel, which held out a similar promise, but which went further and proclaimed the elimination of class barriers.

Both men played a substantial part in transforming the world. But the paths taken by their two nations did not converge after 1919. It was Adolf Hitler who brought them together in a joint endeavour to rid the world of tyranny.

23 Thomas Edison, typical of the technological inventors of America during the great age of industrial expansion, is photographed in his laboratory in 1906.

24 Portrait of Washington, La Fayette and Tench Tilghman at Yorktown,
a painting by Charles Wilson Peale.

II THE PARTING OF THE WAYS

The establishment of a constitution, the founding of a federal republic, enactments relating to land distribution in the West and to the affiliation of new states on an equal footing with the founding states – all these things represented an immense step forward on America's part.

Having declared their independence on the basis of human rights, the Americans had gone on to fight for that independence, and ended by creating a new political community. America was no longer an idea or myth, a hope for the future; it was a new country which had to prove itself in terms of actual achievement within the community of states and nations.

As inhabitants of an overseas province of the British Empire, the Anglo-Americans regarded themselves as 'Europeans', felt like Europeans, and were repositories of western culture. The age of enlightenment had made models of them. Europe was pinning its hopes on the transatlantic offshoot of the human race. There were no nationalist prejudices as yet – on the contrary, the exotic possessed a special attraction of its own. The age of enlightenment was born of a new view of the world, nourished by exploration and tales of travel and supplemented by novel scientific discoveries and insights into the structure of the natural world. In harmony with John Locke's ideas, the Americans had succeeded by means of a 'political contract' – fulfilled in the form of a 'political constitution' and accepted by elected delegates of the former colonies, now constituted as independent communities – in bringing forth a comprehensive modern political structure. They chose as their first president George Washington, erstwhile commander-in-chief in the struggle between the colonies and their motherland, a man who personified dignity, self-control and innate chivalry, and who was the idol of all European votaries of freedom. The question was, how would the new ship of state fare in the unknown waters of the future? 49

America's development at the close of the eighteenth and during the nineteenth century was shaped by the convulsions that occurred in the world of which the new America itself was part, a world set in motion and plunged in turmoil by two revolutions, the French and the industrial. Events in America represented a very important aspect of this upheaval.

The United States sought to go its own way, while simultaneously cultivating the economic and cultural links with Europe which were the mainstay of its existence. The interplay between the United States and the countries of Europe during the nineteenth century, compounded of rivalry and antagonism, support and opposition, was a major feature of the struggle for political power and world leadership.

First, the United States had to work out a line of political action. To the dominant European powers – Great Britain, France, Russia, Habsburg Austria and, towards the end of the century, the new Germany of Bismarck – America was not only an outsider but an enigma. It was not deemed necessary to attach much importance in terms of power politics to what went on there. The crucial factor was the balance of power prevailing between the major countries of Europe, in other words, the concert of powers which had previously included Spain and had been confirmed by the Congress of Vienna.

The French Revolution left Europe in a state of internal ferment. It underwent an intellectual renaissance which manifested itself politically as a trend towards national unity, economically and socially as a transition to industrial society, and in colonial policy as the development of a new colonial system in Africa, the Far East and the Pacific.

The battle of minds took the form of controversy between liberals, conservatives and socialists. The years 1830 and 1848 were ones of successful and abortive upheaval, a continuation of the French Revolution, that is to say, of a struggle against the old class system. Equally convulsive were the Crimean War, the Austro-Prussian War of 1866, and the Franco-Prussian War of 1870–71, for the Crimean War put an end to the Pentarchy, the concept of five great powers working in harmony, and the events of 1866 and 1871 established Prussian Germany's predominance in Central Europe. Meanwhile, in the course of a parallel development, a new Italy appeared on the scene. A radical change in international relations occurred between 1850 and 1870, the period which followed the revolution of 1848 and embraced the years of the American Civil War (1861–65).

25 Thomas Jefferson's design for the façade of Monticello, his home in Virginia. Jefferson was an important advocate of the classical revival in architecture.

It is a striking fact that Germany's rise to ascendancy in Europe ran parallel with America's rise to great-power status, and that Russian expansion eastwards to the Pacific matched American expansion westwards. The Tsarist Empire and the United States were aware that they had many interests in common: as expanding continental powers, they both sought to counter the global influence of British sea-power.

No united front was formed with the new Germany, however, despite tentative moves in that direction. Only a few sage individuals foresaw the possibility of a confrontation between the United States and Germany in two world wars; yet this collision and its results were among the most notable developments in the political history of the twentieth century.

It was tragic that Bismarck's work never underwent constructive development and failed to bring Europe the renaissance that had been hoped for. Instead, the German Empire engaged in a great-power contest for European hegemony in the belief that world domination could be won on the ancient battlefields of Flanders and Poland. The opposite was achieved and 'Europe' receded once more.

26 Overleaf, the US section at the Great Exhibition in London, 1851.▶

A peculiar duality marks the history of the United States during the nineteenth century. Filled with a profound sense of mission, the Americans completed the great task of opening up the West. Although dependent at every stage both on its own exertions and on the more or less benevolent participation of European immigrants, businessmen and nations, the United States discovered the right way to outmanœuvre its European competitors or at least to remain one jump ahead of them. It was finally able to emerge as a great power and assert its determination to play an authoritative part in world politics. The educated classes in Europe failed to comprehend the full significance of this extremely important phase in nineteenth-century history. It was only the coincidence of military involvement that enabled the United States to loom above the European horizon in the role of a great power.

A German historian of the post-war generation, Hans Ulrich Wehler, has recently drawn attention to this failure of Europeans to comprehend the course of events. 'The genesis of the modern world may be described', he says, 'as a history of western society's diffusion across the globe. This expansion should not, however, be construed, as Hans Freyer construes it, as the "world history of Europe", but must include the United States, which ever since the close of the eighteenth century has furthered this expansionary process, in its role as a western society extraneous to Europe.'

It is not necessary to go into the different phases of the political development of the United States, because our study relates mainly to the problem of America's contribution to the history of Europe, to the question of how far it has helped to give the history of the western world another meaning, form and structure.

Even before the war of 1812 against Britain, Americans realized that their future lay in the West. By taking over Canada from the French and adopting their policy of co-operation with the Indian tribes, Britain provoked counter-measures on the part of its own colonials, who were determined to acquire the West for themselves.

Recent American historians have rightly laid emphasis on American expansion in the West as a development which, in terms of migration, land clearance, settlement, conflict with Indians and with nature itself – in short, as a process of territorial annexation and development

27 Daniel Boone, shown here, in a painting by George Caleb Bingham, escorting settlers through the Cumberland Gap, was among the early explorers of the virgin territories beyond the East Coast.

on a vast scale – represents the most grandiose example of modern mass-migration. It should not, however, be forgotten that America's push to the Pacific (like Russia's) was accompanied by violent conflicts with other powers which were equally interested in the process, namely, Britain, France, Russia and Spain. It should also be remembered that there was no unanimity among Americans themselves about the direction and ultimate objectives of such expansion, in particular about the precise extent of the territory to be annexed. Apart from the westward thrust, which only the Indians disputed after the Louisiana Purchase of 1803, there was the thrust to the north. Many Americans regarded the incorporation of Canada as a matter of course. In the south, their gaze was fixed on Cuba and other European island possessions in the Caribbean, and also on Texas, the northern provinces of Mexico and Mexican California.

The acquisition of the vast territorial complex, which had already attained its present dimensions by the mid-nineteenth century, deserves to be assessed politically as a conquest which puts the colonial conquests of the European powers in the shade. Already before World War I, all the territories, being by then sufficiently populated, had been incorporated as states. The population of the United States, at 23 million in the middle of the nineteenth century still smaller than that of France, had risen to 100 million by the time of World War I, and its industrial production already exceeded that of Germany and France together. To Alexis de Tocqueville, gazing into the future, a United States of 150 million inhabitants was the most he could envisage. Today the population has passed the 200-million mark, which it reached in 1967.

The American conquests were wrested, not only from nature, the aboriginal inhabitants and themselves, but quite as much from their European rivals, who were far from acquiescent and had never entertained the possibility that what they had built and acquired in America would be called in question by the United States.

The unrivalled daring with which the Americans set out to create a continental empire, altogether in the style of the European *conquistadores*, may justly be accounted a masterpiece of statesmanlike enterprise. Warlike and military aspects of the process merit as much attention as the diplomatic gambits and *coups* that attended it, because its importance tends to be obscured by emphasis on individual 'pioneering' achievements and successful teamwork on the part of small groups.

28 General Winfield C. Scott enters Mexico City in 1847, during the course of the war which led to a huge increase in US territory.

The wars of 1775–83, 1812–15, 1846–48 and 1861–65, together with the colonial wars of 1898 against Spain and of 1899–1902 against the Filipinos, add up to a very considerable exercise of collective effort in the military sphere. In addition, there were the perennial battles with the Indians, which continued until the end of the century. Of the operations conducted by regular troops under federal supervision against a wide variety of Indian tribes, no less than forty were officially designated wars or campaigns, and some of them lasted for years. The most sanguinary conflict of all, the Civil War, or War of Secession, was an internecine struggle between white men, a confrontation between the Northern and Southern states. It was, in a very real sense, a conflict which had a vital effect on America's territorial future, being directly associated with the preceding war against Mexico (1846–48), which gave the Union the entire region from Texas westwards to the Pacific and northwards to the borders of Oregon, previously shared with Great Britain.

57

29 Recruits in Boston marching off to the Civil War in 1861; a naïve painting entitled *There Shall be no more War*.

The middle of the century saw the Union confronted by a momentous problem. The new West guaranteed the future establishment of a large industrial system on the widest possible territorial basis and gave promise of real world-power status. Acceptance of Southern defection would have amounted to toleration of the existence of a neighbouring state of which it could certainly be predicted that it

would seek the backing of European powers in the event of a conflict. The victory of the North was an event of world historical importance, strangely parallel to the struggle between Austria and Prussia for the creation of a new great power in Central Europe. No one suspected at the time that the reunification of the Northern and Southern states would have such a decisive influence on the destinies of the world 59 during the twentieth century. Instead, Europeans were dazzled by the achievements of Bismarck, who had managed to defeat two great powers in succession and everyone was fascinated by the spectacle of a new European great power in the ascendant.

But the simultaneous rise of the United States was underpinned by resources many times more abundant than those of Germany in respect of land, mineral wealth and manpower. The power of the United States was imperial in scope and character. The trend towards continentalism had never detracted from the country's awareness of being a major maritime power – indeed, intimate links with two of the world's oceans kindled it anew. By the time Germany entered World

30 One of the first naval battles of the Civil War – remarkable for its use of armoured gunboats and submarines – was at Hampton Roads in

War I in search of hegemony, the United States was a generation ahead, and the role of a great world power which Germany had allotted itself merely played into American hands.

During the latter part of the nineteenth century the European powers were engaged in a contest for new spheres of influence in Asia and Africa. Nevertheless, they endeavoured to pursue policies which would not disturb the balance of power in Europe. The Americans, by contrast, behaved as if they were the only major power on the American double-continent. Although the powers of Europe did not formally acknowledge this status, they encouraged the United States to such an extent that it did, in fact, manage to play the dominant role.

1862; a contemporary French lithograph records the scene.

Who was it, it is worth asking, who agreed (in 1803) to sell Louisiana, that is, the entire region extending west of the Mississippi to the Rocky Mountains? – None other than Napoleon Bonaparte. Who (in 1819) ceded the colony of Florida, thereby rounding off the Union's possessions in the south and giving it access to the Gulf of Mexico? – The crown of Spain, at that time still a major colonial power. Who sold Alaska, the continent's north-west flank and bridge-head to Asia, a region equivalent in area to roughly one-fifth of the Union's existing territory? – Tsarist Russia. And finally, who agreed, in the Oregon Treaty, that the outstanding question of the Pacific frontier between the United States and Canada should be settled in such a way that the Union did not suffer, and later that it came off best in the Alaska-Canada border dispute? – The British crown.

Britain did not intervene in the Mexican War even when Texas was forcibly detached from the Mexican motherland and incorporated in the Union. And yet the fruits of victory in the war of 1846–48 included California and the future states of Arizona, New Mexico, Nevada and Utah.

How are we to explain this passivity? What happened in practice was that the European powers were unwilling to disturb their equilibrium on account of America, and would rather see the United States profit than one of themselves. Hence it can be said that the United States benefited because the Europeans were at odds among themselves. At the same time, events in America indirectly undermined the stability of the existing balance of power.

If Napoleon I was prepared to divest himself of his American lands, it was because, while negotiations for the purchase of Louisiana were in progress, he was preparing to become Emperor of the French, and was uprooting the old imperial and ecclesiastical order of Central Europe. He had no time for the New World. When Napoleon III tried to intervene in the liberal-clerical struggle in Mexico, and to profit from the Union's struggle for survival in the Civil War to erect a bastion in Central America – acting here, too, in accordance with Napoleon I's ideas – the result was total disaster. Napoleon had to withdraw his troops from Mexico under US pressure, and Archduke Maximilian, younger brother of the Austrian emperor, who had been installed as Emperor at Napoleon's suggestion, was captured and shot. The prestige of the monarchy suffered a serious blow. Napoleon's blunder meant that the United States, in addition to defeating the separatists at home, won laurels abroad as a champion of republicanism, and that a patent 'infringement' of the Monroe Doctrine was punished in a way that left no doubts about the future.

Of all nineteenth-century colonial ventures, that undertaken by the United States proved by far the most successful, not least of all because it represented a joint European–American enterprise. The contribution made by thirty or forty million European immigrants and a steady flow of European financial aid can scarcely be overestimated, though the United States saw the whole process in a different light.

For them the opening of the West was a great American epic. The strength of isolationism and separatism lay in the fact that they enabled Americans to develop new political ideals and a spiritual patrimony free from European influence, and thus to maintain their purity. It was part of their continuing fight for identity, which had begun during the Revolution with the introduction of a new type of political constitution. In American eyes, expansion in the West represented a new pattern of colonization, a system whereby land acquired and surveyed by the Federal Government was disposed of by auction to speculators (sometimes being given away free to actual settlers), the owners being eventually incorporated in the mother-land as citizens of newly formed member-states in such a way as to interweave colonization with continued national expansion.

31 European immigrants to America in 1850.

At a time when Europeans were re-creating the image of nation-hood out of their past history, Americans saw their adventurous drive westwards as a spur and first step towards a glorious exploit of their own: the acquisition, from coast to coast, of a vast continent, and, beyond that, dominion over the still vaster expanses of the Pacific. This irruption into the 'wide open spaces' was sustained by a belief in progress inherited from the age of enlightenment, and found moral justification in the conviction that it was a task performed for the benefit of mankind as a whole.

The Western Movement was the central event in nineteenth-century American history. This became apparent at the moment when, towards the close of the century, it was realized that territorial acquisition had come to an end and that no further sizable areas in the West remained to be opened up. Frederick Jackson Turner, with the census reports of the Federal Bureau of Statistics in front of him, noted an allusion there to the 'end of the Frontier' and made this the theme of a lecture at the American Historical Association in 1893. Entitled 'The Significance of the Frontier in American History', it saw the secular process of settlement as a development which invested the structure of American democracy with a special character of its own. Turner argued that the fluidity of the frontier – where it was possible to break out of existing society and prove oneself anew in a contest for land with the Indians and with nature – gave the pioneer communities incentive and opportunity to evolve their own form of democracy: one which laid particular stress on equal prospects for all, on each man's chance to acquire land and property, assume personal responsibility and lay claim to political participation. Hence the difference between democracy in the Washingtonian and Jeffersonian sense, which was still 'genteel', and the robust 'shirt-sleeved' democracy later personified by Jackson and Lincoln.

Although his views were later disputed, Turner made an enduring contribution to American self-awareness – one which harmonized with the image of America formed during the enlightenment. But Turner's interpretation also gave due weight to the process of frontier displacement and territorial annexation, as well as to the achievements which the new western states contributed to the national heritage. Turner recognized no problem of class-struggle, but devoted himself at length in later studies to the tensions existing between the various economic regions (sections).

32 A poster of 1890 promoting Western settlement with promises of 'free homes, government loans, and cheap deeded lands' in South Dakota.

In the late eighteenth and early nineteenth centuries, America took its shape, spiritually, from the religious revivalist movement. The puritan heritage (a sense of belonging to the elect by predestination) yielded to an American 'pietism' characterized by confession of sins and conversion. Dietrich Gerhard has shown how religious awakening and American national awareness occurred simultaneously, and has also pointed out that the collapse of the revivalist movement coincided with the constant recession of the frontier. Tocqueville's picture of America embraced religious but not ecclesiastical America; 'voluntary churches' had replaced established religion. A missionary element endowed the revivalist movement with enormous impact and put it – according to Gerhard – on a par with Catholic missions.

33 A pioneer homestead in Nebraska, *c.* 1887.

34 The nineteenth-century Far West re-created in a motion picture of 1968; the stage coach is pursued by Apaches.

By turning away from puritanism and associating itself with the enlightenment's belief in progress, American society blazed a trail to that conception of man's perfectibility which – when catalyzed by modern science, business practice and political organization – was to engender the power structure of an industrialized nation which the twentieth century actually brought forth.

Concentration on action here and now, something not grasped by the church in Europe until a century later, as well as devotion to 'life and works' rather than 'faith and order' – both these were embodied in the unique process of the Western Movement and invested the collective achievements of the United States with a unity which guaranteed success.

35 A view in the Rocky Mountains painted by Albert Bierstadt in 1863. This impression of vast unpopulated areas contrasted sharply with the quick growth of overcrowded industrial sites.

The American myth persisted in the form of a new gospel which preached the dignity of the common man – its greatest exponent was Mark Twain – but the American phenomenon expanded into the concept of 'American civilization'. This expression betrays its provenance from the age of enlightenment. It encompasses the overall picture of the American way of life, democracy, everyday existence, technology, art and religion. The idea of civilization is always focused on the future; it signifies that man is proceeding towards a better hereafter, and that his life serves to bring it closer.

Spencer's evolutionary credo, with its biological and mechanistic basis, its conception of life as a perpetual adjustment between internal and external processes, and its prediction that the world would witness a transition from despotic military tyrannies to pacifist, industrial republics, was adequate to meet the aims inherent in the American vision of the future. Social Darwinism suited the America of the Gilded Age and the coming upsurge of nationalism and imperialism. The élitist instincts of early puritanism lent themselves to incorporation in Darwinist theory. They led, as in Andrew Carnegie and John D. Rockefeller, to the assumption that *richesse oblige*. The vast bequests and foundations which bear their authors' names are tokens of a 'voluntary social work' inimical to the spirit of state paternalism.

Towards the end of the century, the United States was assailed by an intellectual, spiritual and political crisis parallel with the economic depression which affected all industrialized countries in the period after 1873. This crisis found political expression in agrarian unrest, populism and the Progressive Movement. For the United States, engaged in the transition from a predominantly agrarian to a predominantly industrial system, there was something fundamental at stake, because the American myth was closely linked with its unspoiled countryside. Ruthless tree-felling, coupled with the predatory business methods of big bosses (and small) and the growing practice of placing the country's administration in the hands of tycoons from the world of private enterprise, weakened the idea of America as a model for Europe. These new developments might have provided an opening for links with European socialism. What militated against any such development was a native reformism which had more faith in the 69 perfectibility of man and the solidarity of men of good will than in any doctrine of violent upheaval.

It is worth noting, even so, that in this period. Henry Adams conjured up the medieval civilization as an anti-type to the materialist technicism of his own day; even Mark Twain interested himself in the Middle Ages, those days of old which America lacked.

In their effort to evolve a humanism fit for the technological age, the United States and Europe began to join hands. The very loss of 'innocence', or spontaneous naturalness, to which we have already drawn attention, not only shook, but was possibly bound to shatter, the original conception of America. It may also explain why the poetic and literary protest which this loss evoked in the United States had demonic ingredients almost unequalled in Europe, where the age-old urban tradition ensured that conditions were never as starkly contrasted as in America.

The absence of an intellectual conflict which might have set America on the path to revolution is nevertheless a feature which distinguishes it from continental Europe. In this respect the United States remains faithful to British tradition and 'the Great Mr Locke', who was indeed a revolutionary, but one whose revolution had already been absorbed by America. The fact remains that in America as in Europe cultural optimism could be transmuted into cultural pessimism, a trait which demonstrates a capacity for self-analysis and self-criticism and provides scope for liberating action.

The permanent presence of brutality and violence may be another legacy bequeathed by experience of pioneer life, in which people settled their accounts summarily and, as it were, outside society. In so far as society was seen as a secularized religious community, evil was a permanent problem, which concerned the individual rather than the community at large. This meant, paradoxically, that the United States, with its love of reform and experimentation, functioned as an essentially conservative power in a world of permanent revolution. The Adams brothers were well aware of Karl Marx as a revolutionary force; but, as aristocrats, they did not feel drawn to him. The relationship between their ideas and Oswald Spengler's, on the other hand, though not demonstrable in black and white, is so evident that it is easy to see how there could be an understanding between American and German intellectuals on the basis of aversion to the consequences of material civilization.

Few facts were more important in the first century of American history than its determination to remain aloof from events in the rest of the world, ostensibly in order to remain uncontaminated by European power-politics, but actually because the young country was well aware of its own weakness. On the one side was a wish to wield influence in the world; on the other, a characteristic trend towards isolationism and separatism. The latter proved useful as a political principle when, in a later phase, the United States came into conflict with other nations, but its immediate effect was to lead Americans to concentrate on developing what came to be known as the 'American system'.

With the development of the 'American system' the United States drew away from eighteenth-century cosmopolitanism and the free trade which marked the early days of the Union, and adapted itself to the political economy of the late nineteenth century, with its strong mercantilist undercurrents. The demand for a specifically American economic system was tantamount to a policy of thoroughgoing self-sufficiency, and this became possible to implement once the South had been eliminated as a power factor and the agriculturalists had been appeased with the Homestead Act (1862). Industrial tycoons and the great god Business transformed American civilization into a business civilization; and this civilization, as it has developed in the twentieth century, has created – in the guise of the 'military-industrial complex' – a vast computerized technological apparatus which is imperilling the whole historical fabric of American society. This could lead to total anarchy and social dissolution, unless the benefits of the Welfare State are made universally available – in other words, unless technological progress is brought into harmony with the social aspirations of politically emancipated peoples.

If, in contrast to the monarchical, feudal and aristocratic civilizations of the past, the United States continues to concentrate on the 'dignity of the common man', it will be fulfilling its mission in the world and may ultimately establish that long-sought contact with Asia which it feared it had lost after 1949.

The main objective of the young republic's policy, as reflected in the minds of its first presidents, was to secure the country that strong and independent status which would invest the United States with a special character, and put it in a position to contribute to the settlement of global conflicts. Only a profound sense of national purpose can account for the consistency and shrewdness which the Americans displayed in evolving a policy accurately tailored to their country's needs without, at the same time, losing sight of the general aims which they had broadcast to the world in their Declaration of Independence.

Writing in *The Federalist* in 1787, Alexander Hamilton postulated 'one great American system, superior to the control of all trans-atlantic force or influence, and able to dictate the terms of the connection between the old and the new world.' It is astonishing that, at a time when the United States could scarcely be accounted a medium-sized power, an American statesman could so boldly contemplate a policy which has retained its validity until the present day.

The basic axiom of American policy – that 'we should abstain from European affairs' and 'Europe likewise should leave us free' – was propounded at a very early date. Jefferson declared in 1785 that America should behave towards Europe as it did to China. He recognized that, as the 'halfway house' between Europe and Asia, the American continent followed its own law in foreign policy too. However, the nation also experienced a moral obligation and this gave it a sense of mission.

As representatives of a new political system – the federal republic which it was their task to establish firmly on the American continent – the Americans were in possession of an example which they proffered to Europe. It was quickly deduced that the old colonial order was at an end. Being the successors of a colonial régime which had been abolished, the Americans felt justified in demanding that colonialism should vanish from the American continent altogether and leave the way free for them to tackle the task of empire-building *à l'américaine*. In this way they squared the circle from freedom to empire. The Americans now had both a political programme and a good conscience. As successors of the Puritans in a secularized world, they felt called upon, still in the name of God, to embark on the building of an American Empire, and so to complete that policy of colonial expansion which has lured Europeans overseas since the fifteenth century. At this crossroads in history, however, something quite unforeseen occurred.

European colonization did not reach its consummation in America, as the Americans had imagined it would. While the Americans, with their republican gospel, were outrunning Europe, and proceeding to conquer the American continent, the Europeans, too, embarked on a fresh phase in colonial history. Equipped with the instruments of a new technological civilization, they endeavoured to renew and complete the work of the early colonizers. This they did with the same spirit of enlightenment that had caught fire in America and was manifest in the French Revolution, and which later found an outlet in various forms of national revival, in social reforms and in the conservative, liberal and socialist movements of the nineteenth century. The new colonialism was sustained by people of the most diverse convictions and by members of widely different social classes. There were as many reformers at work, not only in the exploration of Africa but also in colonial ventures in Australia, New Zealand and Algeria, as there were reform politicians among the governors-general and viceroys of the British Empire. The opening of Japan by the Americans – who almost lost the race to the Russians – was also part of the western invasion of Asia.

US and European expansion were both based on economic strength revitalized by industrial techniques, and on a conception of progress and evolution borrowed from the philosophy of the eighteenth century. That was why the tidal wave of colonial expansion, as it reached its end, was ineluctably accompanied by demands for liberation and emancipation.

What characterized the United States was its stand against Europe. The French minister Adet, who visited the country in 1796, said of Jefferson that, as an American, 'he cannot sincerely be our friend. An American is the born enemy of all the peoples of Europe.' And Washington's farewell address contains the famous sentence, 'Why entangle our peace and prosperity in the toils of European ambition, rivalship, interest, humor or caprice?'

The guiding principles laid down in Washington's farewell address were confirmed and strengthened in Monroe's annual message to Congress of 2 December 1823, in so far as it advocated the securing of a continental empire and a separate existence for the United States.

In the Declaration of Independence, Americans had professed their faith in humanity; and the idea of a modern republic, strongly tinged with reminiscences of ancient Rome, was expressed in the founding of the Union. The Monroe Doctrine informed the world that prospects for a better future reposed in America, and nowhere else. After Europe had been reconstituted at the Congress of Vienna, and as the main lines of future development became discernible in the years that followed, the Americans, too, clarified their position. Although they wanted no truck with conservative Europe, and were in sympathy with the liberal and revolutionary movements there, they now planned to concentrate all their energies on America. This was the novel feature in the situation.

Previously, there had been a sense of identity with Europeans who aspired to freedom. American influence played its part in the French Revolution and the Americans had conducted a campaign against the Barbary States in the Mediterranean. Jefferson was no stranger to the idea of allying himself with Great Britain and intervening in Europe should Napoleon's plans threaten the United States, and he prepared to do so when New Orleans was endangered in 1802. When, after 1815, the struggle against reaction got under way and engulfed Greece, it was President Monroe who yearned for the liberation of that country and wanted to recognize its independence. John Quincy Adams advised against such a course. America, he said, 'is the well-wisher to the freedom and independence of all. She is the champion and vindicator only of her own. . . . She well knows that by enlisting under other banners than her own, were they even the banners of foreign independence, she would involve herself beyond the power of extrication, in all the wars of interest and intrigue, of individual avarice, envy and ambition, which assume the colors and usurp the standard of freedom.'

After advantage had been taken of European disarray to acquire Louisiana and Florida, and after the Treaty of Ghent (1814) had settled the border with Canada, giving large areas of the Great Lakes region to the United States (without creating the need for a belt of fortifications), this profession of faith in America's separate existence seemed to provide an adequate expression of the postulates of US policy. Metternich and Polignac regarded Monroe's message as an open challenge, but significantly, in Russia and Great Britain, feelings towards the United States differed entirely from those of the continental powers. It was, in fact, the Russians who had promoted the enuncia-

36 The classical influence in a Charleston square, painted in 1872.

tion of the Monroe Doctrine by probing southwards from Alaska towards Mexico, pushing down in the first years of the century to Sonoma county in California, as part of their policy in the Pacific. This was the immediate cause of the veto against further colonial acquisitions. The British, for their part, provided a further reason for President Monroe's declaration by hinting at possible recognition of the South American states which had broken away from Spain. They proposed concerted action, but this idea was rejected. Tsar Alexander was no enemy of the Union, however, and had even contemplated linking America with the Holy Alliance in 1820.

When the United States insisted on non-interference throughout the American double-continent, the Russians at once grasped the possibility of putting pressure on Britain – through the United States – by withdrawing from America themselves. As we can see today, the British were equally astute. By helping to build up America they created a counterpoise against Russia. At the same time, blandly ignoring the Monroe Doctrine, they proceeded to build up a new colonial empire in Canada, which ultimately played an important role as a mediator between Great Britain and the United States, particularly in respect of their interests in the Pacific.

With Britain's dissociation from the policy of the Holy Alliance, Russia's abandonment of its designs on the Pacific coast of America, and the tacitly acknowledged US claim to pan-American hegemony, the policy of colonial restoration pursued by the powers of the Holy Alliance lay in ruins. Latin America followed North America's example. From a practical point of view, the United States emerged triumphant from the turmoil that had marked the years between 1791 and 1815. By dissolving its political ties with Europe, releasing itself from Europe's political past and creating a new political, economic and social system of its own, it was eventually able to become the pivot of the international system in Europe and Asia, and finally, after World War II, the most powerful country in the world.

Nevertheless, intellectually and culturally, educated Americans remained loyal to the artistic traditions of Europe. The United States was soon able, by dint of hard work and the wealth that flowed from it, to assemble collections of European art which now compete with those of Europe. In the end, a Europe in the process of national and liberal transformation unwittingly drew closer to the United States. It should not be forgotten that James Buchanan, when he was ambassador in London between 1853 and 1856, had consorted with Kossuth, Mazzini, Garibaldi, Ledru-Rollin, Orsini, Ruge and Herzen, all exiled revolutionaries. Washington Irving and James Fenimore Cooper, Emerson and Melville, Whitman and Mark Twain, all hoped to win recognition in Europe. They gained a big European readership because their writings incorporated aspects of American life new to Europeans, which captured their imagination.

Once the period of national unification was past and Europe embarked on a new phase of expansion, it was inevitable that it should encounter America again. By the end of the nineteenth century America was strong enough – as it had not been at the beginning – to oppose European infiltration into Latin America, an area which European powers were striving to exploit politically. It even went so far as to expand the Monroe Doctrine by claiming a right to watch over the weaker American republics as a guarantor of their independence. It was successful in enforcing observance of the Monroe Doctrine; but this very success launched it along a road which no longer corresponded with the ideas and intentions of the founders of the Republic.

When the United States burst through the limits of its 'continental empire' and took possession of positions outside – Samoa, Hawaii, the Philippines – which its whole previous political tradition forbade it to lay hands on, the result was collision, confrontation, and finally embroilment in those very quarrels, wars and intrigues which Americans had hitherto thought typical of Europe, and to which they preened themselves on being immune.

Admittedly, America still did its utmost to avoid Europe, to sever connections with Europe, turn its back on Europe and build a new world of its own devising. But the very success that attended its efforts to become a great nation by its own independent endeavours meant that in time of European crisis, disarray and dissension America stood ready to play the 'saviour'.

What gave America its chance was the European crisis. It is no accident that the two super-powers of the twentieth century are nations which have remained true to the spirit of the enlightenment and which have embraced the idea of progress with a messianic fervour far surpassing that of other countries. This is why, by creating a technological civilization which none of us can escape, they have succeeded in bending the world to their leadership.

CULTURAL
EXCHANGES

37, 38, 39, 40 Right, Jules
Verne was attracted by the
United States as a land of the
future; this illustration of a
flying machine in the Rocky
Mountains is from his 1886
novel, *Robur le Conquérant*.
Below, Charles Dickens and
Oscar Wilde were two
popular literary figures who
successfully toured the
United States. Opposite,
Manet's lithograph for Poe's
The Raven.

41 Right, Henry James, the expatriate American novelist, painted by John S. Sargent, the expatriate American artist.

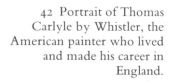

42 Portrait of Thomas Carlyle by Whistler, the American painter who lived and made his career in England.

43 Opposite, this portrait of Mrs William Page by her husband (1860) illustrates the American traveller in Europe, her cultural outlook symbolized by the ruins of the Colosseum in the background.

OUT FOR A FIGHT

Rear Admiral SAMPSON on the Bridge of the "NEW YORK"

III CONVERGENCE AND DIVERGENCE
1890–1940

Between 1890 and 1940 the United States emerged from its isolation, reached for and eventually secured a sphere of influence during World War I which extended as far as Central Europe, and then demonstratively returned into its shell. In 1940–41, with the advent of World War II and the involvement of the Pacific area as a result of Japan's thrust into South-East Asia, it resolutely accepted the challenge of Pearl Harbor and, as we shall discuss in the next chapter, established itself as the paramount world power, with Washington D.C. as a world capital.

The initial phase, during which the United States pushed beyond its continental boundaries into the Pacific and to Asia itself, was marked by preliminary encounters and clashes with European imperial powers which regarded the same area as their own particular preserve. Differences were resolved by international agreements and by the distribution of colonies in accordance with the normal practice of power politics (1889–99 Samoa, 1898 the Philippines, Hawaii, Guam). In World War I, however, after a long period of waiting and hesitation, the United States made a positive decision to intervene, revealing by its deployment of military, maritime, financial and political resources its intention to have a voice in re-shaping the political order. The United States proclaimed its mission with the same clear voice as Russia, which was then treading the path of revolution. Just as the latter hoped that revolution would spread to Central and Western Europe and, when this failed to materialize, was thrown back on its own resources, so the United States withdrew from Europe politically after Versailles (1919) and adopted a policy of extreme isolationism during the 1930s, a period when Russia was again beginning to play an active role in international politics.

In reality, however, the policy of isolation could not hide the fact that the United States had greatly strengthened its position in the

44 The United States Navy as an instrument of imperial expansion (1898).

system of powers, both politically and economically. It built up a regional treaty system embracing the whole of the American double-continent and the Pacific, which was really a sort of 'second front' complementary to the European-centred League of Nations. The Kellogg-Briand Pact of 1928 forged a link between the two systems. During the late 1930s the United States found itself confronted anew by the international responsibilities which it had sought to avoid, and World War II committed it on all fronts to such an extent that it could no longer divest itself of the leading role, though its desire was to share it with Russia.

Between 1890 and 1940 the United States took on a new appearance. It grew into a giant economic power, established an industrial system based on steel, coal, electricity, natural gas and petroleum, and built up a communications system which is still a shining example to the rest of the world. In addition to developing its domestic market, it moved vigorously into international commerce and the capital market. Nothing more drastically revealed the revolutionary change in world economic conditions than the fact that the European great powers – hitherto purveyors of capital to America and supreme in all the world's markets – were gradually ousted by, and became heavily indebted to, the United States. In fact, it was indebtedness to the United States and the coupling of this indebtedness with the problem of war-debts and reparations after World War I that was the root cause of world economic instability from 1914 onwards, and that helped to bring on the worldwide economic crisis of 1929–32; this in turn promoted the events that led to the National Socialist dictatorship and, ultimately, to World War II.

Having abandoned its detachment – its 'isolationism' – under the pressure of events and moved to the centre of the international stage, the United States exercised a powerful, if not decisive, influence over the course of world politics. During the previous four centuries world history had been dominated by Europe; from 1917 onwards the impulses which have given the contemporary world its distinctive appearance emanated from Russia and the United States, Europe's flanking powers.

The way the changes came about was very singular. Already at the time of the revolution in communications the European powers had begun to exert economic and political influence over the economically backward and culturally stagnant areas of the world – Africa,

Asia, the Pacific, South America; they established colonial empires there and proceeded to divide the world into spheres of interest. International trade fostered an exchange of commodities and capital between the industrialized countries and primary producers supplying agricultural products and raw materials, as well as between the industrialized regions themselves. In turn, industry furnished world commerce with the necessary media of communications – telegraph, telephone, radio technology, and finally, earth satellites – which created a communications network encompassing the entire globe.

The age-old European struggle for power shifted perceptibly to the non-European world and led to a race for colonies, protectorates and spheres of influence. Overseas expansion at first decreased internal tensions within Europe. Once the world had been divided up, however, conflicts on the periphery were bound to make themselves felt at the seat of power, the metropolitan area of Europe. This was clearly perceived by the Germans in particular, who, having fared badly as last-minute runners in the colonial stakes, saw a chance to improve their position in the event of conflict.

But the future held a prospect of something more fundamental than merely another redistribution of colonial possessions and a rearrangement of spheres of influence. Because European expansion was to a large extent an economic and social process, and because the less developed agricultural and trading countries were drawn into the wake of the technological revolution, the political leaders in the dependent territories seized upon the new system of values that stemmed from Europe. European influence provided the impetus for a worldwide trend towards emancipation.

Just as there was an internal Social Darwinist trend in western countries which helped the lower classes to improve their status, so there was an imperial Darwinist trend which led to international competition and arms races on the part of the naval and military establishments. The next stage was the cry for liberation from the European yoke in the colonial world which had been subjugated by Europe and drawn into the nexus of world trade.

We can see today that the two world wars, the Russian Revolution of 1917 and the American decision to intervene in Europe, the Great Depression and, finally, the Chinese Revolution, which was the epilogue to World War II, were not only sanguinary and catastrophic upheavals, but were also milestones in the vast process of 85 transformation leading from the modern to the post-modern era of world history.

The roles of the actors in this continuing historical drama may be defined with some degree of precision. As the mistress of an empire, Great Britain saw the process whereby imperial power was relaxed and finally relinquished as an opportunity to steer the mutual adjustment of the colonial and European worlds into peaceful channels. The Empire became a commonwealth of white and 'coloured' peoples invested with equal rights. Great Britain's consistent application of this policy eventually made it the advocate of the black Africans against its own white brothers, not that this astonishing feat saved the British from a disastrous decline in international influence. Britain lost its world-power status because two global wars, both of which it had sought to avoid and neither of which directly affected the mother-country except in the form of aerial warfare, debilitated it so much that it was sucked into the back-wash of the super-powers.

Germany faced the new situation with a romantic blend of traditionalism and faith in the marvels of technology and organization, obsessed with the idea of imprinting its own image on the world. The attempt to create German world power by means of a carefully planned military strategy twice set off a chain reaction of armed intervention which shattered the world's traditional international system and helped to promote social revolution.

Europe's self-destruction paved the way for the rise of the two flanking powers, Russia and the United States, to the rank of 'super-powers'. World War II also opened China's path into the future and turned the Pacific into a 'Mediterranean'.

Political amity reigned almost continuously between Russia and the United States during the nineteenth century, because both powers recognized Britain as their chief adversary, and sought to shield one another against the British by a policy of reciprocal concessions and tokens of mutual respect. With the incipient heightening of international tension, however, and in consequence of the westward shift in US spheres of influence across the Pacific, Russia came to be regarded as a competitor, and sometimes even an opponent. We can already discern here the rudiments of the post-1945 Cold War polarization. The latter was, of course, engendered by conditions in Western Europe, but it was over the question of China that serious friction first arose between the two countries.

45 Commodore Matthew Calbraith Perry meeting the Japanese Imperial
Commission during the expedition (1852–54) of the American Squadron
to Japan and the China Seas.

At the close of the nineteenth century the Chinese question kindled
and shaped the political antagonisms and friendships which were to
characterize international relations throughout the ensuing period.
All the great powers planned to get something out of China, which
seemed in the heyday of imperialism to offer the greatest opportunities and a major market. France established itself on the edge of
the colossus by building an Indo-Chinese empire designed to beam
influence in China's direction. Others – the British and, later, the
Germans – sought to acquire territorial concessions in the 'Kingdom
of Heaven' itself, and planned to develop them into spheres of interest.
As an Asiatic great power, with the whole of Siberia under its control,
Russia aspired to sovereignty over north-east Asia and to the incorporation of additional Chinese territory. To the United States,
China was a trading partner of long standing. It developed into a 87

46 A view of the American Methodist Mission's compound in China, 1893.

favourite area for American missionary activity and increasingly became the field of operations for a genuine 'civilizing mission'. Apart from building churches and hospitals, the Americans founded colleges, and ultimately invited the cream of Chinese students to study at their own universities under bilateral agreements. The revolutionary movement in China developed under the spell of European and American political thought, until at last, after a twenty-year struggle, Mao Tse-tung gained power and freed his country from the foreign yoke. Armed with a home-made version of communism, he succeeded in ranging Maoism alongside the communism of Marx and Engels and Lenin and Stalin as a revolutionary ideology of equal status, and thus introduced China to the world as the leading power of the future.

Although the communist revolution undermined its influence in China, the United States still saw China as a country with immense potential. President Nixon's initiative in 1971 picked up threads which had been woven in the nineteenth century. China is, after all, still America's infinitely populous neighbour across the Pacific, still – as it was in the past – America's greatest historical object-lesson. The

United States had desired to break away from Europe and to become active in Asia. Even in early times, the China trade was its particular concern. And it was in China towards the close of the nineteenth century that the United States encountered the European powers which it had avoided in Europe.

The Americans sought to follow a political line of their own in China – not the 'isolationist' policy which they pursued towards Europe, but a parallel operation attuned to the policy of the other powers. It was not long before they felt themselves to be champions of China's integrity. Of course, at this stage Japan was a far more important partner. The Japanese had twice won sympathy, first during the war against China in 1895–96, and then during the Russo-Japanese War of 1904–5, because each time Japan was regarded as an under-dog which merited good wishes in its fight against a hostile 'colossus'. After 1905, however, the situation began to change. Japan now strove for leadership in the east as Germany did in the west. Both nations cherished the hope of acquiring a predominant role in their sphere of influence similar to that of the United States on the American continent.

Even World War I, in which Japan sided with the United States, was indirectly brought about by Japan – though by a Japan which had enjoyed British support since 1902. Had it not been for the weakness which Russia revealed to the world in the Russo-Japanese War, the German Empire would never have dared, nine years later, to risk the possible consequences of going to war with Russia and France simultaneously. Again, had it not been for the Great Depression, which disclosed America's weakness, Japan would not twelve years later have joined Italy and Germany in the Tripartite Pact and launched the attack on Pearl Harbor in 1941.

Russia's penetration of Manchuria after the Boxer Rebellion prompted the United States to commit itself in China. Later, it was Japan whose encroachments on China during World War I caused the United States to sponsor a collective Pacific and East Asian policy. It was Japan's greater East Asian policy during the 1930s that confronted President Franklin D. Roosevelt with the choice between abandoning China and risking a conflict with Japan. Japan's problem in relation to the United States was precisely similar. The outcome was a drama which, in terms of its setting (the Pacific and East Asia), the number of men involved and the nature of weapons deployed, may be 89 regarded as the most grandiose and earth-shaking spectacle ever mounted within the space of a few years (1941–49). The first act was Pearl Harbor, the last act Hiroshima and Nagasaki, and the epilogue the People's Republic of China – in other words, a new China which detached itself from both the United States and Japan.

The two world wars involved America in a struggle to both west and east and cast it in the role of 'the middle continent', a role which it had really wished to avoid. The United States was fated to discover that there is no salvation in isolation. Its isolation was not respected, so it resorted to intervention, but even that afforded no escape. It may be America's task as the middle continent to become, instead, a global mediator.

AMERICA'S IMPERIAL HERITAGE

As we trace the stages by which America rose to world-power status, we are brought face to face with the question of American 'imperialism'. American tradition had it that no such thing ever existed, for the simple reason that America's emergence into history during the War of Independence was construed as an act which precluded any belief in imperialism. By rebelling against the authority of the British crown, the colonials proved to the world at large that they were capable of independent action outside the Empire, and thus demonstrated the futility of imperial power. So much for popular convention. What of reality?

The Americans waged war against George III's government as British citizens, and they were supported and encouraged in their venture by the Whigs, who were no denigrators of the British Empire. The word and concept 'empire' was quite as current among the British on the other side of the Atlantic as it was among those in the United Kingdom, and the idea of the Roman *respublica* and *imperium* remained their model.

Prior to 1776 Washington, Jefferson and Franklin were American British. They reproached the British in Europe not for their imperial aim of steady and continuous aggrandizement but for aligning that policy with the requirements of the British crown and ruling class. But they remained so British that, once freed from the yoke of Westminster, they pursued the same policy in America – with a somewhat different emphasis – as the British of England. They spoke of their 'imperial republic'. Washington took part in the campaign to conquer Canada in 1776. Jefferson, once the Treaty of Paris had allotted the eastern Mississippi region to the United States, cast an acquisitive eye westwards.

The Americans, like the British, looked upon Central America and the Caribbean as part of the North American area. Hamilton observed that, with the Caribbean in their pocket, the Americans would be the arbiters of the world, because almost every colonial power had colonies there. Franklin employed the terms 'nation' and 'empire' as identical; in the view of the distinguished historian R. W. van Alstyne, he was an imperialist like Pitt. Jefferson, an opponent of the principle of a strong central government, took over Louisiana from Napoleon and, by this single act of territorial expansion, reinforced the Union's power more than any article of the federal constitution could ever have done. The United States followed Britain by perpetuating the practice of territorial expansion, the only new feature being the framework of the republican constitution. This allayed any niggling doubts that expansion might be inconsistent with the principle of a constitutional state. There was constant talk of 'our Federal Union' in the period that preceded the American Civil War. Once the Union had withstood this test of cohesion, Americans happily spoke of 'expansion' and 'empire'.

The problem of US imperialism is bound up with the question of Western migration and was associated with Turner's theory of the frontier and its importance as a determining factor in American cultural development. The imperial element acquired a missionary inflection in the slogan, dating from 1845, of Manifest Destiny. Having gained currency at the time of the annexation of Texas and the tussle for Oregon, this assumed the nature of a watchword in face of the surprisingly swift penetration of the West, which was considered – or claimed to be – 'providential'.

In retrospect, the 'period of migration' came to be contrasted with an imperialist period deemed to have begun with the war against Spain in 1898. In reality, however, the vision of a country which embraced the entire continent, Canada and Central America included, hailed from the colonial era, and was carried over into the nineteenth century by the Union. In the same way, the theory of 'continentalism versus sea-power' fails to accord with the actual course of events. 91

47 A cartoon by Thomas Nast, 1867, on the purchase of Alaska from Russia. It was thought to be a foolish waste of money at the time, and was called 'Seward's folly' after the Secretary of State who arranged the deal.

48 American and British fleets at anchor in 1868, in the port of Hyogo (now part of Kobe), at a time when Japan was beginning to have relations with the west.

Despite undoubted fluctuations, sea-power was never neglected. In the Civil War, the North defeated the South largely because of its superior sea-power. The Mexican War of 1846–48 was an amphibious war prosecuted with the aid of naval forces in the Gulf of Mexico and along the coast of California. Indeed, California was 'conquered' from the sea. The Southern states always had an eye on Cuba, as well as Puerto Rico and Nicaragua. Acquisitions in the Caribbean area were constantly being considered during the first half of the century and mooted in the Senate, but they did not go through as long as the question of slavery remained unresolved. Once the Civil War was over, the paramount task was to unlock the West. This was more than a colonizing process. Its consequence was the Union's transformation into a mining and industrial nation and its further progress towards imperial status.

Parallel with the race across the continent to the shores of the Pacific was expansion across the Pacific itself. Like the abortive

Ostend Manifesto, which envisaged the annexation of Cuba, the first treaty with Japan was dated 1854. In 1867, Secretary of State William Seward, a great imperialist, secured Alaska for the United States from Russia, which was anxious to get rid of so exposed a territorial outpost. Admittedly, the purchase was so unpopular ('an inhospitable, wretched and God-forsaken region worth nothing') that the Tsar's ambassador had to distribute bribes in order to get the treaty past the Senate.

New England missionaries had first set foot in the Hawaiian islands as early as 1820. In 1875 American sugar-planters signed a trade agreement, and the United States acquired a naval base in the Samoan islands (provisionally in 1872, permanently in 1878). Agreement was reached with British and Germans in 1889 on a three-power condominium there, but the United States had already secured the island of Tutuila and its fine harbour (Pago Pago). Midway Island had already been acquired in 1867 as a station on the sea-route to Japan, 93 and in 1886 a South Pacific base was acquired in the Tonga Islands, on the route to New Zealand.

Nothing demonstrates more clearly how closely the Americans followed the pattern set by the British, both in maritime and continental policy, than the 1868 trade agreement with China. The United States was reaping the benefits of the west's two wars against China in 1841–42 and 1858–60, and unhesitatingly became a party to the treaty system which the western powers had substituted for the existing system of tributary payments. The Chinese Empire was transformed into a multilateral protectorate with a multiplicity of guarantors.

In spite of these earlier precedents, the year 1898 was undoubtedly one of considerable significance. At the end of April the United States declared war on Spain, a European colonial power. The war very quickly went America's way and was terminated in December of the same year by the Treaty of Paris. It was a war by sea and land, in and off Cuba, in Puerto Rico, off Manila (and subsequently in the Philippines themselves until 1902). The fruits of victory comprised the Philippines and Puerto Rico. Thereafter, Congress resolved to annex the Hawaiian group of islands, together with the islands of Guam and Wake, as intermediate bases on the route from Honolulu to Manila. The protectorate over Cuba (1901) served strategically to secure and consolidate the United States' newly acquired dominance both in the Caribbean area and, later, by protecting the Panama Canal, in the Pacific. The victory of Manila Bay and the conquest of Manila itself were an indication to the United States, now that its position in the Pacific had been reinforced, that it could take a more active part in Chinese affairs.

In his book, *The Great Experiment*, Frank Thistlethwaite describes the period between 1890 and 1920 as a time of grave internal American crisis. It may equally be regarded as a vast new 'departure', whereas the years between 1920 and 1940, though signifying a fresh start in the economic sphere, were politically an era marked by the re-examination, revision and reconsideration of what was deemed to have been an aberration from America's rightful path.

In my view, the era of the Spanish-American War, of Theodore Roosevelt, Taft and Wilson, was a time of fulfilment. I do not concur with Turner, who taught that the end of the frontier was the beginning of a period of uncertainty. As we have seen, trans-continental expan-

94

sion was always matched by naval activity, and it seems clear that the thrust into the Pacific was envisaged from the beginning as a continuation of the advance across the continent – indeed that it went parallel with it. It began with the operation of sealers, whalers and merchantmen whose sails were later superseded by belching funnels, the mysterious advent of which prompted the Japanese to unveil themselves to intruders from the outside world.

To be sure, the new departure was an upheaval too. Nineteenth-century America was an America of regions – East, South, West, and their subdivisions – whose relations have aptly been likened to those of social classes in Europe. With the 'end of the Frontier' the American continent coalesced into a single unit linked by an increasingly dense network of communication. The continental empire now resorted to its only instrument of power, the navy. Turner was a contemporary of Admiral Mahan and, although their junior, of the brothers Henry and Brooks Adams. Mahan and the Adams brothers left their readers in no doubt that the world was entering an American era which – true to the new style – they hailed without enthusiasm but considered to be ordained by fate. It is disturbing to find Brooks Adams expressing the hope that the European empires would not collapse too rapidly so that the United States would have time to arm. The Adams brothers had no faith in Germany's future greatness or in the permanent world-power status of Britain (for which Brooks Adams predicted a socialist future); instead, they sensed what far-seeing men had predicted long before, namely, the coming greatness of Russia and the United States.

Mahan was, and is, the great mentor of all devotees of sea-power. As such, he could not fail to be an upholder of British tradition. He dreamt of an Anglo-American maritime condominium, and that implied a common policy in the Pacific. Britain was already the leading power there. Its position was not only buttressed by an alliance with Japan but founded on the colonial endeavours of settlers, largely of British stock, in Australia and New Zealand, and on the possession of numerous Pacific islands. Brooks Adams regarded China as the major objective, and it was the struggle for China that prompted him to call for increased American military preparedness. Here, he believed, lay America's chance to become the greatest power in the world.

All these factors provide an indication of how America's sudden leap to world-power status should be assessed.

It is important to distinguish between 'colonialism', 'dollar diplomacy', and considerations of military defence and strategy.

Historians speak today of 'formal' and 'informal' empire. In America's case, the distinction is of fundamental importance. Strategic interests – in other words, considerations of military security – do not always accord with the aims of politicians. Admiral Mahan did not regard the acquisition of the Philippines as essential, nor did he call for their conquest. He wanted Manila as a trading and coaling station, a commercial base; it was not his ambition to turn the whole archipelago into a colonial possession. All those who were interested in trade with China – i.e. the representatives of big business and many politicians – believed that control of Manila would give them the necessary counterpart to Singapore or Hong Kong, a key to the gate of the Far East.

It is easy to understand the belief in the need to build up a strong position in the Pacific and confront the European powers in the Far East with a policy tailored to US interests. Mahan demanded, as a strategic principle, the consolidation of the Atlantic and Pacific fleets. In other words, he called for the building of the Panama Canal. With the intervention of 1898 against Spain, the conquest of Puerto Rico, the construction of the Panama Canal (after safeguarding a 'Canal Zone', by fomenting a revolt in the republic of Colombia); with the annexation of a chain of islands extending diagonally across the Pacific to the Philippines, and the laying of a cable across the Pacific Ocean; with a naval construction programme which only the British were allowed to surpass – in short, with this display of power, development of communications and acquisition of bases, the United States laid the foundations of a policy equivalent in importance to the Monroe Doctrine: the 'Open Door' and the maintenance of China's territorial integrity.

It was a policy which, far from aiming at possession of a colonial empire, was designed to foster trade and secure uninterrupted commercial expansion. It was an answer to the 'end of the Frontier', a breath of fresh air after two gloomy decades of economic depression.

We know that Secretary of State John Hay's notes on the Open Door question were drafted in close consultation with British political figures. Hay had previously been US Ambassador in London, and

49 Building of the Panama Canal, one of the linchpins of US world strategy.

his adviser during the preliminary work was an associate of Robert Hart, the Englishman who had built up the Chinese customs service. At the time of the Boxer uprising, when fresh territorial concessions (on 99-year leases) were granted to Germany, Britain and Russia in the Yellow Sea area, and when Russia was threatening to burrow deeper into Manchuria, the United States based its intervention in China on the principle of free trade. The Americans, too, had entertained the idea of leasing a territorial base at Sansa Bay, situated further south in the province of Fukien, opposite Formosa, but they dropped the plan when informed that it would be unacceptable to Japan. Thus, the United States was perfectly placed to urge the powers with territorial concessions to pursue a non-preferential policy under which Americans would be granted the same trading rights as their 97 own businessmen. The postulate of 'China's integrity' was an adjunct to this policy.

In the four ensuing decades, the United States tried, in collaboration with Britain and, more especially, with Japan, to develop a Pacific and Far Eastern policy under its own leadership, the prerequisite being that naval supremacy in the Pacific be shared with Britain.

The 'free trade principle' might suggest that the United States wished for, and secured, a big economic stake in China. This, as Brooks Adams indicates, may once have been the intention. In practice, the Americans led the field neither in commerce nor in capital investment. They were predominant in the missionary field, in medicine and in higher education. It has already been pointed out that China taught them the 'historic dimension' which they ignored in their confrontation with Europe. At any rate, American museums and private collectors probably possess the cream of China's art treasures, and Buddhism claims a relatively large number (some 200,000) of adherents in the United States. The waiving of half the Boxer indemnity (1908) enabled a Chinese college to be opened, and between 1911 and 1927 more than 10,000 young Chinese were sent to study at American universities.

Under Presidents Theodore Roosevelt and William Taft, the US administration tried to interest American businessmen in China to a greater extent than their business interests warranted. This was done in order to 'consolidate' the avowed policy of free trade, and was an attempt to prevent other nations from acquiring railroad and mining monopolies in contravention of the aims which the United States had set itself. It was in this sense that in 1909 Secretary of State Philander C. Knox proposed a 'neutral' railroad undertaking.

In the period following World War I the United States tried to accomplish in the Pacific what the League of Nations had failed to do in Europe. The Washington Conference of 1921–22 may almost be described as a repetition, under Republican Party auspices, of the Versailles drama; what was more, substantially the same powers took part, with the United States indisputably cast in the principal role. The three main subjects under discussion were naval strength, the integrity of China, and the question of island possessions. What was at stake politically was the balance of power in the Pacific; ideologically, the issues were disarmament and collective security. Since the

United States was by now becoming the premier naval power

in the world, it was able to steer the conference its way by offering to join in limiting naval construction. The proposal for parity
between the fleets of Great Britain and the United States was a step
towards the fulfilment of one of Mahan's basic ideas: the collaboration of the two largest naval powers in the world. The demand that
Britain should abandon its alliance with Japan was in line with a new
collective policy which eschewed bilateral pacts. Thus the Hay
doctrine of the Open Door and Chinese integrity was now anchored
in the nine-power agreement relating to China.

The ending of the Anglo-Japanese alliance undermined the basis
of previous Japanese policy and left no alternative – at least in the eyes
of leading military and political circles in Japan – save to go it alone.
This change in the direction of Japanese policy was signalled by the
occupation of Manchuria in 1931. The Far East, and Japan in particular,
once more became the centre of a convulsion which affected Europe
too. There is a striking parallel here. Substitute Germany in the west for
Japan in the east, and we encounter the same process: frontier changes,
abrogation of treaties, violation of the spirit of agreements. Japan
ignored the treaties designed to preserve a free China, Germany the
limiting clauses of the Versailles treaty.

The western powers had a unique opportunity to make Manchuria
a test case and, by taking joint action with the United States, publicly
to demonstrate the existence of the community of peace-loving
nations which the Kellogg-Briand Pact had envisaged. No such
drastic measures were agreed, however. Preliminary consultations
with the United States took place in the security council and a US
representative was heard on the subject of the Pact, but no joint action
resulted. In practice the United States retained leadership, but its
conduct did nothing to strengthen the common front of the western
powers. Instead, true to the spirit of Woodrow Wilson (who had
employed the device of non-recognition in 1913 against the murderers
of President Madero in the case of Mexico), Secretary of State Henry
Stimson resorted to the same principle, thereby making all too
plain the purely verbal nature of US protests and stressing America's
determination to follow an independent line of its own (1932).

The United States did not, it is true, stick to its policy of pure
abstention when the Japanese proceeded to occupy the central provinces of China and set up a puppet government. China was excluded
from the Neutrality Acts of 1935–37 so that it could be supplied with

arms. The US government also permitted the recruitment of the volunteer flying teams which aided Chiang Kai-shek against Japan at a time when the Chinese communists, too, were collaborating with him in resistance to the invader.

It followed logically from the stance adopted by the United States, which consisted in turning its back on Europe and pushing doggedly westwards, that, when the challenge to battle came, it was from Japan in the Pacific in 1941, not from Hitlerite Germany in the Atlantic in 1940.

THE CLAIM TO HEGEMONY IN LATIN AMERICA

Let us now turn to US policy on the American continent and its attitude towards Europe, and see what light it casts on 'US imperialism'. There is no doubt that the United States pursued a genuine policy of power and sought hegemony within the American continent. Here its claims to a privileged position relative to all other countries were based on the Monroe Doctrine. In this area at least, it is probably fair to see a close similarity between American attitudes and theories of imperial obligation, the imperial mission, the white man's burden put forward at the same time by European power.

The United States felt called upon to maintain order throughout the whole continent. Theodore Roosevelt not only expounded such ideas but put them into practice. We have already referred to the acquisition of the Canal Zone. Roosevelt is also said to have been instrumental – as Assistant Secretary of the Navy – in dispatching Admiral Dewey's squadron from Hong Kong to Manila Bay when war was declared on Spain. He participated personally in the Cuba campaign, and his prestige as a 'war-hero' partly accounted for his elevation to the Vice-Presidency under McKinley. The fact that he became President after McKinley's assassination in 1901 and was confirmed in office in 1904 meant that he directed policy for nearly eight years.

An ardent disciple of Admiral Mahan, Theodore Roosevelt was the first to call unequivocally for United States participation in world politics. He personified the new great power from across the Atlantic. But wielding influence in the world was not his sole concern; what mattered to him was that the United States should be recognized as a power with a mission of its own. And in this he was successful. He gave numerous demonstrations of the United States' claim to the status of a world power and won the recognition he sought. This success was confirmed by four notable events: US mediation at Portsmouth, New Hampshire, between Russia and Japan at the end of the Russo-Japanese War (1905); the American fleet's round-the-world tour (1908–9); participation in the Algeciras conference on Morocco (1906); and the award of the Nobel Peace Prize (1906).

Roosevelt reformulated the Monroe Doctrine so as to cover US action in Central America and the Caribbean and to earmark that area as a special preserve of US influence (the Roosevelt corollary to the Monroe Doctrine, 1904). There had already been two previous occasions relating to Venezuela (1895 under President Cleveland, 1902 under Roosevelt himself) on which the world had been given to understand that the United States considered itself the sole champion of the small American republics.

Just as the Open Door policy was the main thread of US policy in the Pacific area, so the Monroe Doctrine governed policy in Latin America. The Monroe Doctrine had originally been a warning against would-be European intervention in the American fight for independence, coupled with a declaration that America had its own particular approach to life and political organization. The fundamental aim was to secure political and military guarantees of the United States' own independence, and that of its Latin American neighbours. But once the United States developed into a great power and won a dominant economic position, a new motive came into being. The aim now, while penetrating the double-continent economically, was to transform it into a secure bastion of US power by the establishment of a pan-American system.

It is clear that the United States had no wish to see rivals operating in the Caribbean. The British, who far surpassed all other colonial powers in this area by reason of their naval strength and the numerous islands in their possession, recognized this and relinquished the lead by concluding a new Panama agreement and conceding US naval superiority in the area, at the same time as the United States was giving them a helping hand in the Far East by means of its Open Door policy. At the beginning of the twentieth century the Caribbean region became an American sphere of influence complete with protectorates (Cuba, Nicaragua, Haiti, Santo Domingo), colonies or territories (Puerto Rico, the Canal Zone), and naval bases (Guantanamo in Cuba,

Fonseca Bay in Nicaragua). In October 1914, after world war broke out in Europe, President Wilson opened the Panama Canal.

The United States' debouchment into world politics was largely a consequence of its continental policy. The double-continent was the nearest and most logical training ground, and the weaknesses and strengths of US policy were products of experience gained in that area. The failure to develop a military organization on a par with its status as a great power can be traced to the military weakness of the United States' immediate neighbours. It has been asserted, probably with some justification, that the ease with which the United States rose to power (for lack of external foes) may have accounted for the fact that it was 'pampered' and had no adequate conception of the problems posed by the power that had, as it were, dropped into its lap. As a dominant power which wished at the same time to be an exemplary one, the United States developed the instruments of a policy of hegemony, but coupled it with a policy of continental solidarity, which found expression in the Pan-American Union and later in the Organization of American states.

The idea of a pan-American union originated among Bolivar's associates, but the Congress of Panama (1826) did not bring about the understanding between North and South that had been planned. The principle of the Monroe Doctrine prevailed. The subsequent Pan-American Union was the outcome of endeavours to form an American economic union launched in 1889 by Secretary of State James G. Blaine. At a later stage, an attempt was made to unite the American republics in a collective organization for peace (with reciprocal pledges of non-intervention). The external threat to America in the two world wars eventually brought political standpoints in the North and South closer together. During the inter-war period the United States undertook a revision of its Latin American policy and dropped the presumptuous claims advanced by Theodore Roosevelt. Franklin D. Roosevelt inaugurated the 'Good Neighbor' policy, which re-nounced the principle of armed intervention and sought to strengthen pan-American solidarity. In those years, the United States gave up its protectorates, proposed political independence for the Philippines, granted the Puerto Ricans full US citizenship and eventually offered them the right of secession, which they declined.

The United States won its reputation as a promoter of legal pro-cesses in the sphere of international law by settling innumerable inter-

50 Uncle Sam in the guise of a schoolmaster trying to teach independence to his charges: Hawaii, Porto Rico, Cuba, the Philippines (1898).

American, European-American and European-Asian disputes and by making itself the advocate of a system of arbitration agreements (many of which failed to secure Senate approval). It also caused a stir at the Hague Peace Conferences of 1899 and 1907 by championing an Argentinian jurist's proposal that any sanctions implemented against debtor-nations by means of armed force should be declared to be in contravention of international law.

An examination of US Pacific and pan-American policy supplies us with a provisional answer to the problem of US imperialism. The United States was not equipped to build a colonial empire because it lacked the prerequisites. It never possessed a colonial ministry. What was more, US colleges never produced an élite corps of colonial administrators, civil or military, nor were there many would-be emigrants prepared to go overseas.

The islands which the United States gained were fruits of victory, spoils of war and – with the exception of Hawaii – colonies acquired at second-hand from other colonial powers. At once, controversy arose over the question of how they should be treated without contravening the principles of the constitution. The answer in principle was precisely as the territories on the American continent had been treated – in other words, as aspirants to the status of member-states with full and equal rights.

The colonies were immediately granted 'representative government', but Congress retained executive and administrative authority over them. As territories belonging to the Union, colonial acquisitions were granted the same economic status as the United States itself. The hope of reversing this decision was one of the chief reasons why business interests wished to restore independence to the Filipinos, and why the Filipinos rejected it until agreement could be reached on a transitional arrangement, which led in 1946 to complete independence. Alaska and Hawaii joined the Union after World War II as the 49th and 50th states respectively. Puerto Rico has since 1952 been a 'self-governing commonwealth freely and voluntarily associated with the United States'.

It is clear that strategic considerations underlay the acquisition of the small Pacific islands, just as they were the reason, for example, for the purchase of the Virgin Islands in the Caribbean from Denmark in 1917, for the sum of 25 million dollars. Often, it was a case of 'preventive annexation', of positions which were judged to form part of the American defensive system and were bought up to prevent their falling into foreign hands. If the United States renounced colonial sovereignty after the first flush of enthusiasm at the turn of the century, this was because it was in a position to build up an 'informal' empire unencumbered by administrative costs. Americans made their major investments in the neighbouring countries of Canada and Mexico. The new industrial economy of the United States imported raw materials from Latin America and Asia and supplied those areas with manufactured goods; commercial exchanges with Europe declined in percentage terms. This accorded with a policy of economic expansion, not one of territorial conquest on a grand scale, which would only have produced wider areas of friction. The United States was a continental country which strove for mastery of the seas as a basis for worldwide trade.

We must bear this in mind as we turn to the problems arising from World War I.

INTERVENTION IN EUROPE

When we turn to Europe, we at once encounter quite another political climate. Here, the old and well-established principles of the Monroe Doctrine still applied: non-intervention and detachment – 'we have a different political morality'. That, indeed, had been the deeper significance of the Open Door notes: if they denoted a *rapprochement* with the European powers for the purpose of penetrating the Far East – in other words, a convergence of interest – American policy nevertheless followed an independent line. The United States had even agreed to a condominium with Great Britain and Germany in the case of Samoa, and had joined in the deliberations at Algeciras. When war broke out in 1914, however, Americans of all persuasions were determined to have no part in that. They saw it as confirmation of their traditional view that Europeans were incapable of abandoning their Machiavellian intrigues: hence their continual embroilment in a succession of bloody wars.

There is no need to discuss US policy between 1914 and 1917 – neutrality, the principle of freedom of the seas, the wait-and-see policy and ultimate involvement in the war. What concerns us is whether the common experience of war in 1917–18 brought the United States and Europe closer together, how the victory of the western powers altered the existing power structure, and what conclusions were drawn therefrom.

Perhaps the most important consequence of the two world wars was that relations between the United States and Europe, often muted during the previous century, moved to the centre of the international 105 stage. We can see today that what passed between the United States and Europe during the period 1917–45 was one of the most dramatic and impressive developments in recent history, and yet its significance was in no way fully appreciated. Influenced by their traditional ideas, Americans failed to relate their own achievements to the changes wrought in the international scene by the United States itself, and were slow to come to terms with reality.

The period is full of paradoxes and contradictions. Americans clung to the idea that they wanted nothing to do with European wars, even after they had in fact fought in Europe and had largely determined the outcome of the struggle. They tried to dismiss the fact of their involvement because the war was not an American war, and had not been started by them. Accordingly, they withdrew into an isolationism which was no longer really feasible because, for good or ill, they had committed themselves, economically and militarily, and allied themselves with Europe – a fact for which they simultaneously wanted due credit.

In his proposals for a peace settlement announced both to the belligerents and to the whole community of nations, President Wilson enunciated a global political programme which was intended to mark the beginning of a new era. His plan was based on ideas which may be described as typically American: the principle of national self-determination and the idea of an international 'covenant', in other words, of voluntary co-operation and the subordination of members of the League to a jointly constituted leadership.

Welcomed by public opinion in Europe, in some quarters with enthusiasm, this programme was rejected by the Americans, or, rather, by their Senate. The European powers had incorporated the Covenant of the League of Nations in the Versailles Treaty at American insistence, the organs of the League were set up and Geneva was chosen as the headquarters of the new institution – and then the United States declined to join. However, it participated in some conferences, e.g. those relating to disarmament, and was on the verge of joining the International Court. None of these ventures was successful except the naval disarmament agreement, concluded at the 1921 Washington Conference, which functioned initially, although all that survived of it in the 1930s was a bilateral Anglo-American agreement.

In Wilson's policy towards Europe we can discern a third variant of US foreign policy. We have already stressed the contrast between

51 James Montgomery Flagg's post–World War I poster suggesting the special relations between Great Britain and the United States.

the policies pursued in the Pacific and the Far East, on the one hand, and in North and South America, on the other: in the former case, policy was focused on sea-power, trade, and the acquisition of maritime strategic bases; in the latter, the United States practised a thoroughgoing policy of hegemony, exercised tutelage over smaller states, and sought military security and safeguards against European interference. In Europe, where great industrial powers were locked in bloody strife, different aims and methods were obviously called for.

Seeing the world war assume ever greater dimensions and drag on towards an uncertain outcome, Wilson at first tried to end the catastrophe by means of a negotiated peace ('peace without victory'). After Germany, miscalculating the odds, had not only supplied the United States with a pretext for intervention but positively provoked it by waging unrestricted submarine warfare, Wilson put forward his Fourteen Points, a project for a new world order under international law which he sought to realize in practice by attending the post-war peace conference in person. Wilson's journey to Europe – the first to be undertaken by a serving American President – was rapturously received by the masses. Having returned home, he was struck down

52, 53 The Peace Conference of 1919. Left, crowds in front of Maxim's restaurant in Paris welcoming President Wilson; above, detail of Sir William Orpen's painting of a meeting at the Quai d'Orsay.

by a severe illness while touring the country to win support for the League of Nations project, and never recovered. This made it easier for Wilson's political opponents in Congress, and the upshot was that they refused to ratify his handiwork.

Once again, as at the time of Theodore Roosevelt's interventions, foreign policy became a central theme of political debate. Roosevelt and Wilson were both internationalists in their own way. Roosevelt had visions of a US empire with worldwide influence, Wilson of a United States whose mission was to bring peace to all nations. Roosevelt chose the method of 'go it alone', and even under Wilson the United States remained only an associated power in the war; but at Paris in 1919 he fought for a new collective international system.

A 'go it alone' policy may take the form of imperialist expansion or national isolation; its ultimate expression is 'Fortress America'.

Likewise, a policy of 'co-operation' may be either aggressive and offensive, or pacifist and anti-militarist. In the period extending from the presidencies of Theodore Roosevelt to those of Franklin D. Roosevelt and Harry S. Truman, the United States experimented with all these variants, applying them in different ways in different regions (Asia, America, Europe) and in accordance with the problem on hand (e.g. the insulation of California against the 'yellow' races, at the time of American expansion across the Pacific).

What the United States sought in its exchanges with Europe was 'identity', or at least understanding for its political actions. The lamps had gone out all over Europe in 1914. It seemed that Wilson was the man to light them again – that America would bestow new hope on Europe.

Wilson's intervention in the conflict between rival European powers might appear to have been an innovation in the foreign policy of the United States. But one has only to recall the War of 1812–14 to realize that this was not so, and it is noteworthy that the 1812 conflict was also occasioned by a threat to the freedom of the seas. Thus it represents a striking parallel to the events of 1917, even though it was fought in America. The Monroe Doctrine did not provide for a war fought on European soil, but Wilson was invoking ancient tradition when he summoned the United States to join a crusade for freedom. To the liberals of Europe his coming seemed like a fulfilment of the American dream in which writers of earlier generations had indulged.

Wilson's aim was to join with Europe in concluding an international pact and establishing a league of nations. The diplomatic intrigues inherent in the old system of balance of power were to be replaced by a system of 'open diplomacy', a public dialogue among nations. Struggles for power would be transformed into political debates among national delegates in the halls of the League. Only with such a prize at stake did Wilson consider it justifiable for the United States to abandon its isolation.

The Paris talks soon showed, however, that, far from bringing about a *rapprochement* between nations and the men who represented them, war and the fight for survival had heightened nationalist sentiment and international antagonism. Nevertheless, the responsibility for letting slip a momentous historical opportunity must be shared between the Senate and Wilson himself, who was a stubborn man. If Wilson's policy was criticized for being too idealistic and illusory, the policy of his opponents was quite as vulnerable to the same charge. Though the United States made little effort to accommodate countries which were deep in debt and suffering from war damage, it offered Germany no alternative to the Allies' peace treaty, but merely (in 1920) declared the war with Germany to be at an end, resuming diplomatic relations with a Germany that had been whittled down in size by the Paris treaties and was encumbered with a still unspecified war debt.

RETREAT FROM EUROPE

Despite its withdrawal from the scene, the United States was from 1920 onwards a power constantly to be reckoned with by Europe, which was heavily in its debt. In 1917 America had come to Europe with its armies, relying on its undisputed sea-power. Thanks to its naval strength, the U-boat blockade had collapsed without the loss of a single troopship; thanks to its economic strength, the Allies had been supplied with arms, foodstuffs and manufactured goods. Although the USA dissociated itself from the Versailles Treaty and refused to join the League of Nations, American policy had undergone a complete change of tack.

We have already described how the United States seized the lead in the Pacific, shifted the balance of power in its favour by means of 'Equal Partnership' (i.e. the claim to naval parity with Britain), and drew closer to the British Dominions in the Pacific by urging and securing the termination of the Anglo-Japanese Alliance.

The essential thing now was to clarify US relations with the European powers. Just as the nineteenth-century policy of going separate ways had been succeeded, in the imperialist age, by a policy of working on parallel lines with Europe, so the reaction to Wilson's policy of intervention and global involvement was a phase of intensified withdrawal. Isolationism was the term used: instead of pursuing global policies, the United States was to revert to the time-honoured principles of earlier years and concentrate on its domestic affairs. It was to isolate itself, shield itself against a world which had proved, once again, that it was quite as degenerate as the Founding Fathers had always claimed.

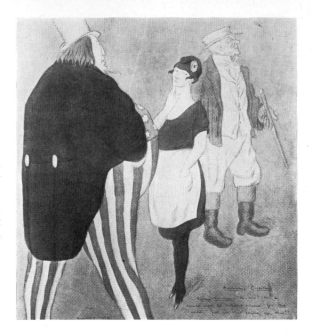

54 Max Beerbohm's cartoon, *Marianne's Creditors*, shows an aggressive American asking for repayment of debts before the 'too dellacut-minded' Briton.

But isolationism in the nineteenth century, at a time when the United States was a small or medium-sized country and effectively enjoyed the protection of the British fleet, was very different from 'isolationism' at a stage when it wielded economic power, naval supremacy and the influence peculiar to a creditor nation. This new isolationism was in no sense a primary or spontaneous development in US policy. On the contrary, the United States had demonstrated to the world that it possessed the dimensions and status of a world power. If Americans now spoke of isolationism, it did not, and could not, mean total withdrawal, but was simply the cloak, donned in response to opinion at home, for a global policy dedicated to extreme nationalism under the isolationist banner.

The dual nature of US policy is clearly illustrated by the reparations problem. By insisting on the fullest possible repayment of war-debts by its late allies, the United States exerted a decisive influence over the whole issue of reparations. Nor, from another aspect, did it help to liberalize world trade, but rather pursued a national and protectionist policy to the detriment of the world economy.

Although fundamentally opposed to participation in the reparations policy adopted by the victors at Versailles, the United States

55 The unpopularity of 'money-bags' United States. This German cartoon of 1924 by T. T. Heine is entitled *Master of the World*.

insisted on concluding with its debtors repayment agreements designed to ensure that it would be financially reimbursed for consignments of arms and foodstuffs delivered during what had, after all, been a joint struggle against a common foe. The debtor nations pointed out that they themselves would be unable to meet their obligations if Germany failed to pay reparations. What was surprising was that the United States, instead of rejecting such arguments, co-operated with the Allies in their policy. It appointed senior experts – General Charles G. Dawes and Owen D. Young – and made itself responsible for arranging terms of payment when the reparations systems eventually was organized. More than that, the final outcome of the whole reparations and inter-Allied debt repayment process was that the United States once again – as in the war – advanced most of the requisite funds: in short, it financed German economic recovery so as to enable Germany to pay indemnities to the victors, so that the latter would in turn be able to meet their obligations to the United States.

The role played by the United States was not a particularly happy one. On the other hand, the Europeans could hardly reproach the Americans for a determination to collect their dues because it was they themselves who, by forcing the Germans to accept responsibility for an unspecified indemnity and then imposing heavy reparations, created a major obstacle to the revival of international trade. Economic considerations would have required Germany to pay off its debts by means of export surpluses, but no other country was willing to envisage this because they were all afraid of transforming their own economy into a debtor economy by excessive imports. The United States – itself the leading creditor nation – led the field in adopting a protectionist policy. Despite its accession to power and greatness, it clung to the mentality of a debtor nation.

Although they had thus taken over economic leadership from Great Britain, the Americans failed to develop the qualities that had enabled London to become the world's financial metropolis. They did, of course, differ from the British in possessing what amounted to a world market within their own continent. Foreign trade played a very small part in their economic life relative to internal American trade; Britain, by contrast, was a country which could survive only if it maintained close and active commercial links with the outside world. Hence, not surprisingly the transition to thinking and acting in terms of a world economy came hard to the Americans. During the war, it is true, that they had associated themselves economically

56 This breadline in San Francisco in 1931 became a familiar sight throughout the United States during the depression.

with the western powers, but in the post-war period divergences again arose. The wartime *rapprochement* never matured into genuine co-operation but led, instead, to a retreat into the American shell. Far from opening its markets to foreign trade and taking the lead in a policy aimed at dismantling trade barriers, the United States paradoxically committed itself to economic isolationism. Ten years after the war ended, the western world underwent the greatest of all depressions, a disaster which brought about the collapse of the international monetary system and led to a régime of quotas and bilateralism – in other words, to exchange control and the bankruptcy of the existing system of worldwide multilateral free trade.

The Great Depression may fairly be regarded as the epilogue to World War I. The breakdown of the existing political system was confirmed by economic crisis. If it had not broken away in 1919, the United States might possibly have wielded greater influence over the economic settlement of the war. Instead, it retired from the scene and, fascinated by its own unprecedented boom, manœuvred Europe by remote control into a position of economic dependence. European gold payments and shipments produced an imbalance in monetary policy. The gold did not help the United States, nor was it used to import more foreign goods into the country and so ease the position

There's no way like the American Wa

The use of this Poste donated by Foster and Kleiser

of foreign debtors. The only reason the system managed to survive so long was because the United States granted Europe further loans until its own collapse brought this flow of funds to an end.

A veritable breach between the Old and New Worlds resulted. The Hoover Moratorium was a final attempt to save the system, but the collapse spread from America to Austria, Germany, Britain and, increasingly, to parts of the world which had hitherto traded with each other on a relatively unrestricted basis. Coupled with the setback to countries producing agricultural goods and raw materials, where the slump had first set in, this seemed to confirm that, far from having overcome the disastrous effects of a global war, the world had entered an era of continuing crisis.

Depression spread everywhere, intellectual and spiritual as well as economic, and Europe did not hesitate to take it out on the United States. At the Lausanne Conference (1932) the whole reparations system was more or less annulled and the United States was informed that, as a result of the depression, its European debtors were no longer in a position to make further repayments. Great Britain made a few more token payments, but only little Finland continued to meet its obligations in full.

People in the United States felt that they had been duped. US–European relations hit rock bottom. Everyone now knew that the lamps had indeed gone out and that no one would help to light them again. Each country proceeded to put its own house in order as best

57 Nationalism on the American highway billboards of 1937.

58 John Steinbeck's novel *The Grapes of Wrath* (converted in 1940 into a successful film, from which this still was taken) presented a rather truer picture of America's economic ills.

it could, according to its own ideas. The victors too now suffered defeat; the vanquished enemy of 1918 took his revenge. The Germans could hardly be blamed if they now set out to build a new order. Not only had US credits enabled them to restore their currency, but by the time the reparations balance sheet was complete they turned out to have received more than they had disbursed! Chancellor Heinrich Brüning declined to solve the unemployment problem by deficit spending and bequeathed the task to Adolf Hitler. Thus the Führer was given a good start and the opportunity to consolidate the Nazi régime. The drastic methods he used are notorious.

On the plane of world politics, Hitler did not possess the stature which Germany needed if it were genuinely to transcend its past. In this respect *Mein Kampf* is singularly informative. Hitler gained wide support for his proposed revision of the Versailles Treaty because even the victorious powers now realized that the settlement of 1919 had failed to produce the anticipated results. However, the fact that concessions were now made to National Socialist Germany which Weimar Germany had been refused gave some indication of the extent to which apathy, resignation and, ultimately, the spirit of defeatism had spread among the western powers. The League of Nations, to which Germany was admitted in 1926, and from which Russia had provisionally been excluded, might have provided a platform for expounding and launching a European policy. The beginnings were there in the form of the Locarno treaty and Briand's European plan, 117 but success did not attend Briand's project, though his idea of following up Locarno by reconciling France and Germany was inspired by ideas which later, in the days of Adenauer and de Gaulle, proved to be wholly practicable.

The only practical result of Briand's initiative was the Pact of Paris, or Kellogg–Briand Pact. This agreement was a formal attempt to outlaw war; but, lacking formal sanctions, its results were nil. It has however, considerable bearing on our discussion for it shows that, even during the 1920s, the Americans did not feel exempt from a duty to co-operate in preserving peace. The United States played a leading part in the General Disarmament Conference held at Geneva in 1932, even though it was not a member of the League of Nations. Thanks to the success of the London Naval Conference of 1930, which was intended as a continuation of the Washington naval disarmament talks of 1921–22 and which appeared to guarantee further co-operation among the three Pacific powers, Japan, Britain and the United States (France and Italy declining to co-operate because they were unwilling to accept any restrictions on their policies in the Mediterranean), the United States felt emboldened to make its mark at Geneva as a peace-keeping power. Then came the Manchurian affair and, with it, a turn in the tide of world events. There followed Germany's withdrawal from the League of Nations (1933) and Japan's repudiation of the naval agreement (1934). Hitler's renunciation of the Versailles Treaty and the Locarno Pact (1935–36) were symptoms of radical change and showed that the victors of 1918 were losing their grip on international developments.

THE SEARCH FOR A NEW IMAGE

The trials which it had been forced to undergo eventually prompted the United States to take a different view of its 'identity' and mission, notably in regard to Europe. This process amounted to a revision of the attitude and outlook which had held good for more than a century.

Once the failure of Wilson's attempt to convey America's message to the world was acknowledged, Americans began to have doubts about the values which they had hitherto cherished. Besides, the face of twentieth-century America differed from that of the early days. Those who called for adjustment to the circumstances of the twentieth century were acknowledged to be right. Feeling that they had been rejected by Europe, the Americans sought new ways of stressing their Americanism and national character.

The thesis of the 'end of the Frontier' had provided the slogan for a change of direction. The United States was no longer virgin territory for an endless stream of immigrants to settle in, yet it was since the closing of the frontier that immigration figures had risen to record heights. New arrivals settled in the cities, and the racial characteristics of southern and eastern Europeans were far more obtrusive there than in rural areas, where an equally chequered assortment of immigrants – Scandinavians, Swiss, Germans – had settled down among or alongside each other. Pleas for the control and selection of immigrants, which had already been raised before the war, acquired even greater force once the war was over.

The new immigration laws, enacted immediately after the war, signified a genuine farewell to the American past. The United States was no longer, nor could it be, the Eldorado of the persecuted, the refuge for those who had been hounded out of Europe, the land which gave each man a second chance – if, indeed, he had ever been granted one in the first place.

The 'melting-pot' theory received a new interpretation. Ellis Island, the transit camp or quarantine station for dubious immigrants, became the symbol of another United States. It had previously been thought that there was room for all in the American melting-pot, that the genesis of an 'American' was a process which had the widest possible variety of ethnic roots. The concept which now operated was that of a standard American, the prototype being what has more recently been called the WASP, or White Anglo-Saxon Protestant. All endeavours were to be directed towards preserving this standard type by means of a selective immigration policy which as far as possible kept out unwanted ethnic groups and based admission on a 'qualitative' quota system. This trend towards Anglo-Germanic racialism is clearly demonstrated by the fact that, in computing the quota allotted to individual countries, the 1921 law based itself on the 1910 census, whereas the law of 1924 fell back on the census of 1890, a year in which the influx of 'new immigrants' was barely under way. The aim of this measure was to preserve the ethnic structure of the old colonial and agricultural America.

This was easier said than done, and for various reasons. In the first place, the war had cut off the flow of European immigrants, with the

'THE PROMISED LAND'

59, 60 Jewish immigrants from Russia arriving in New York, 1892; below, Ellis Island in the harbour, where immigrants went through rigorous examination.

61 Immigrants
photographed in 1896
at Battery Park, where
they would have
arrived after being
passed through Ellis
Island.

62 Right,
a scene from Charlie
Chaplin's *The
Immigrant*.

result that the Negro reservoir of the South opened for the first time, and black workers flowed in large numbers into the towns and industrial areas of the North. Secondly, the nurturing of good relations with Latin America and Canada dictated that preference be given to Americans from the North, i.e. Canadians, and from the South, i.e. Latin Americans, as well as to inhabitants of US colonial possessions, once they had been granted full citizenship. (This did not, of course, mean that concessions could not be annulled by a series of 'administrative' interventions and decrees, as in the case of the Mexicans.) In later years, during the rise of the new European dictatorships, the United States regained some of its reputation as a haven for refugees by giving sanctuary to immigrants from all the totalitarian states, not on a mass scale, it is true, but in sizable quotas. This influx, which included men like Albert Einstein and Thomas Mann, Enrico Fermi and Niels Bohr, brought the United States some prominent intellectuals who not only contributed greatly to its world image, but were instrumental in helping their adopted country to succeed in World War II.

It was only natural that World War I should have stimulated and strengthened national sensibilities in the United States as elsewhere. It has often been pointed out that the first-generation American identified himself far more strongly with his land of origin than he had previously been aware. People in the United States, too, had also been split by the war into factions which debated whether or not to enter it, and what form intervention and the peace treaties should take. These symptoms had to be combated. The United States was now a nation with an image of its own – one which it was desirable to preserve. During the nineteenth century, remoteness from Europe had been a shield against inundation by European influence. After the war, in an age when the continents were drawing closer together, additional safeguards had to be built in. It was thought that, in self-dedication and allegiance to isolationism, the United States had found the national idea which met its needs, a means of regaining the inner stability which it had lost by venturing into a futile war.

Renewed withdrawal from Europe was a symptom of the changed mental climate of the post-war period. Americans again sought some sort of refuge in the traditional American idea that they were 'better people'. Yet they had measured their strength against Europe. The opposing forces of convergence on Europe and of divergence from

63 Jennie Jerome, the American heiress, who married Lord Randolph Churchill. Their eldest son, Winston, is at right.

Europe held the scales in balance. The United States adhered to the trend which had led to the national state in Europe by deliberately cultivating its own 'heritage', as Turner had insisted it should. The fostering of nationalism, clearly exemplified by President Herbert Hoover, went hand in hand with a high-tariff policy which conflicted sharply with the role that had fallen to the United States as a creditor nation. The country which enjoyed an unprecedented boom in the 1920s, which underwent a technological revolution, which accomplished the transition to the age of electricity, petroleum, natural gas, radio, 'talkies', the automobile and the aeroplane, which established New York's Stock Exchange as the financial hub of the world – this was the country which now whipped itself into a lather of forced nationalism.

Relations with Europe were ambivalent. As members of a mature and now wealthy nation, Americans enjoyed the respect of Europeans. Marriages to American women, notably heiresses to vast fortunes, were in vogue in England even before the end of the nineteenth century. Still earlier, an American woman named Mary Esther Lee, who became, in turn, Princess of Schleswig-Holstein and Countess von Waldersee, had played a striking role at the Hohenzollern court in connection with William II's first political moves. Jennie Jerome, Winston Churchill's American mother, is alleged to have had a great influence on her son. Consuelo Vanderbilt married the Duke of Marlborough, and thus made possible the restoration of Blenheim Palace. Lord Curzon, too, married two American wives.

The brilliant American portraitist John Singer Sargent, more at home in Florence, Paris and London than in the United States, painted 123

64, 65 The visit to
New York in 1860 of
Edward VII when he
was Prince of Wales
(above, the grand ball
given in his honour)
was echoed in 1929
when the Prince of
Wales who became
Edward VIII was
fought over by New
York Society matrons
(left).

66 Right, Sargent's
portrait of the Duke of
Marlborough with his
American heiress wife
(Consuelo Vanderbilt)
and two children, 1905.

67, 68, 69 Above, Ezra
Pound is seated on the left in
this painting of Vorticists in
a London restaurant. Right,
the American Sylvia Beach
with James Joyce in the door
of her bookshop in Paris.
Opposite, Picasso's *Homage
to Gertrude*, 1909, in honour
of the American expatriate
Gertrude Stein.

British and American celebrities. America's 'lost generation' of the 1920s found a home in the Latin Quarter of Paris. A sense of their own maturity prompted its members to seek intimate contact with Europe rather than shun it; even if they did not behave particularly as Americans, they had something to give as well as to receive.

Like Russia, the United States became a problem to Europe in the 1920s and 1930s. Having fended off the threat of communism in Central Europe, the Europeans needed American help in order to survive the post-war period. The United States finally made it possible to check the continuous inflation of the mark by helping to finance Hjalmar Schacht's consolidation plans with a huge loan. It also backed the stabilization of currency in general. Its prosperity in the 1920s favoured the restimulation of world trade and a rise in living standards, but no solution was found either to domestic social inequalities or to the international balance of payments problem until Wall Street collapsed and the subsequent worldwide economic crisis necessitated a new attitude and different approach.

It was at this time that Russia launched its experimental five-year plans and Hitler implemented a programme of pre-financing which banished unemployment and, step by step, transformed a planned economy founded on bilateralism and operated by means of currency manipulation into a war economy which was geared to conquest, not solvency. In John Maynard Keynes, England possessed the fore-most exponent of modern economic theory and a practical financier, who also advocated a system of government pre-financing in the interests of full employment. This the United States took over in the New Deal under the designation 'deficit spending'.

In the New Deal, the United States likewise committed itself – albeit reluctantly – to planned economic objectives, in other words, to a centrally controlled or manipulated system of the sort adopted more or less consistently by all the national economies that had been thrown back on their own resources after the collapse of international trade and the money market. Centralization, economic planning, quotas, protective tariffs, devaluations and a tendency towards autarchy all went hand in hand.

The period of transition from Hoover to Franklin D. Roosevelt and the return to a Democratic administration had a truly cathartic effect. Every effort was made, particularly in Europe, to play down the New Deal. It was emphasized that it was no revolution, that nothing had fundamentally changed, that some of the new economic planning bodies had been thrown out by the Supreme Court, and so on. Viewed in the context of US-European relations, the New Deal was nevertheless a turning-point of great and fundamental importance. The question as to how far it constituted a 'revolution' may be answered in advance by the fact that – as the author himself witnessed – Americans felt it to be one, even if it was not what would be called a revolution in Europe. Even in the United States it did not amount to a total upheaval. Superficially it was no more than a change in the ruling party, but Roosevelt was determined to give his policy a different appearance from Hoover's. He was able to draw his proposals and innovations from the reservoir of populist social and economic reforms, which – it is worth recollecting – had themselves been fed by the currents of European social policy and socialist reform, though populism had so far enjoyed little success in fulfilling its aims. With 129

70 Norris Dam in Tennessee, one of the many federal projects undertaken in the early days of Franklin D. Roosevelt's administration.

Roosevelt came a time of fulfilment. With him too, especially in the late 1930s, came a re-emergence of Wilson's legacy.

If, seen from Europe, the inter-war period was a time when European hegemony collapsed and the roles of the United States and Europe were reversed, this was possible only because of the cathartic effect of the upheaval of the years 1932–34. 'We had been cheated of our uniqueness', observes Daniel Boorstin. America's sufferings were the sufferings of Europe. It was no longer the land of escape but, on the contrary, the *fons et origo* of the Great Depression – to many, indeed, the author of the whole catastrophe.

In Germany, as a result of popular indignation at mass poverty, Adolf Hitler rose to become leader of the German people. Russia, though recovering economically by dint of its five-year plans, was paying for this cure with millions of human lives; Stalin resorted to purges which eliminated the majority of first-generation revolutionaries and subjected the Russian people to a reign of terror without precedent. Roosevelt was a charismatic leader-figure endowed with the personal dominance of Wilson, Theodore Roosevelt and Lincoln. With this political temperament at the helm, the United States was well equipped when the time came to resist the dictators and uphold the American cause.

Hoover blamed the Europeans for America's economic crisis and traced it back to the inferno of World War I, itself a product of Europe's despotic past. Of Roosevelt it is known that he picked envoys from among his closest associates and sent them to Europe so that they could report to him on measures taken there to combat the crisis, on socio-political and financial innovations. We thus find elements of British and Swedish prototypes in the New Deal housing and social security programmes, borrowings from Germany in the programme pursued by the Agricultural Adjustment Administration (AAA), and similar borrowings from Denmark in the educational programme of the Tennessee Valley Authority (TVA). Even so, the New Deal was a reform in its own right and bore the trademark 'Made in USA'.

It is clear that fundamental changes took place in the agricultural sector, in the control of stock exchanges and banks, in labour legislation and, subsequently, in the trade union movement. The important thing was that there had been a display of visible and all-embracing government intervention in economic life – an irreversible process, the result of which is that today everyone expects the state to intervene when crisis looms in unemployment, inflation or the balance of payments. This may on occasion lead to greater instability than before, but it does mean that the state feels or is held responsible for the course of economic activity, whereas earlier generations expected crisis and depressions to be dealt with by the 'market mechanism'. Europe took particular note of this. Roosevelt operated with a 'sense of state'. This was a great change. The concept of the 'state' in the European sense had never existed in America. It was Roosevelt's brilliant gift to be able to invest his compatriots with civic awareness and unity through the medium of his radio 'fireside chats' and gain their acceptance of his ideas.

Conversely, the New Deal won adherents in Europe. It is significant that Léon Blum's policy was hailed in Europe as 'the French New Deal', even if, apart from the theory of purchasing-power, the policy of the Popular Front had little in common with Roosevelt's directives and administrative agencies, later abandoned in part. Similarly, Canadians nicknamed the policy of their Conservative prime minister 'Bennett's New Deal'.

In 1933 both Keynes and Bernard Shaw announced with all possible emphasis that they were pinning their faith on America. In an open letter to President Roosevelt, Keynes wrote, 'You have made yourself the trustee for those in every country who seek to mend the evils of our condition by reasoned experiment within the framework of the existing social system. If you fail, rational change will be gravely prejudiced throughout the world, leaving orthodoxy and revolution to fight it out.' By establishing his 'Brain Trust', Roosevelt lent respectability to the 'eggheads' or intellectuals. Keynes regarded the President's collaboration with a team of welfare economists (of whom many, e.g. Rexford Tugwell and Raymond Moley, came from Columbia University) as a token of Roosevelt's experimental approach. As he said in a broadcast in 1934, 'Theoretical advice is being taken by one of the rulers of the world as a basis of large-scale action.'

In the same year a group of young reform-minded British politicians, Harold Macmillan among them, extolled Roosevelt's bold measures and regretted that they were being ignored in England, where Ramsay MacDonald and Philip Snowden had, in fact, remained true to classical financial policy while Roosevelt was experimenting with his deficit budget. In Belgium Paul van Zeeland, a Princeton graduate and former teacher at Johns Hopkins University, who formed a multi-party cabinet in 1935, was criticized in the same year for following too closely in the footsteps of Roosevelt's New Deal. The President of Mexico congratulated Roosevelt on his large-scale programme for the relief of unemployment, and messages expressing friendly solidarity with Roosevelt's venture came from other Latin American countries. The economic crisis and the struggle to resolve it robbed the United States-Europe antithesis of its meaning. Everyone was in the same boat.

THE NEUTRALITY ACTS

Little of this, however, was detectable in the field of practical politics. On the contrary, it is quite clear that Roosevelt's administration led the country on to heights of nationalist jingoism. One has only to note the attitude of the US delegation at the London Economic Conference of 1933, which was, of course, a necessary consequence of Roosevelt's devaluation of the dollar. For a country with vast gold reserves this devaluation was in no way essential from the point of view of the balance of payments. It was, in fact, simply intended to prime the economic pump at home by producing a price spiral which would stimulate market activity. Roosevelt's action wrote *finis* to the whole story of reparations and debt agreements. There was no need to keep faith with a Europe which failed to honour its agreements with the USA. America could live without the rest of the world and was determined to prove it.

As we have already seen, it was economic crisis which engendered the national resurgence that was to hold the world in suspense. In America, things took a dramatic turn. There were Americans who shared Roosevelt's desire to give their country a further chance, but only if – now that mistakes in domestic policy had been corrected – blunders in foreign policy were also put right. They wanted to reinforce the withdrawal into isolation by laying down irreversible norms for the maintenance of neutrality.

In the fire of self-purification which was a concomitant feature of the New Deal, the Nye Committee was set up to investigate how the United States had come to take part in the Great War at all – and this almost twenty years after the event. With the grim perseverance of flagellants, in a climate of social reform and total pacifism, the committee reported that intervention had been founded on the most sordid of profit motives, that Wall Street had had its finger in the pie, that the object had been a wish to safeguard the repayment of loans by entering the war on the side of those to whom most had been lent, and that – in sum – no such thing must ever be permitted to happen again.

A start was made by passing the Johnson Debt Default Act (13 April 1934), which banned financial transactions with governments that had failed to discharge their debts. The Neutrality Acts of 1935, 1936 and 1937 were intended to preserve the United States from the danger of involvement in future European wars. It was hoped to achieve this end by renouncing the freedoms that had given rise to conflict in World War I: US citizens were prohibited from travelling on ships belonging to belligerents, US ships were forbidden to carry military cargoes, and the United States would no longer permit deliveries of munitions and war material to belligerent nations. Moreover, the President was granted the right to decree, on his own initiative, additional, more drastic measures designed to protect the United States still further from involvement in future conflicts.

But this was exceptional. In general, the policy of Congress during the critical years of the late 1930s was to curtail the President's freedom to conduct foreign policy, so as to bring important decisions under its own control. This display of mistrust in Presidential management of foreign policy culminated in a resolution sponsored by Representative Ludlow of Indiana on 14 December 1937, calling for a constitutional amendment which would make any declaration of war subject to a national referendum. The proposal was rejected, but only by a relatively small majority. Against a background of mounting crisis – the Abyssinian War, the Spanish Civil War, Munich, Poland – the isolationists made a last vigorous effort to preserve America's innocence and shield it from infection by European bacilli. It was a field-day for US nationalism, which represented as grave a danger to the world, despite its different nature, as blinkered imperialism.

That a great nation, for fear of involvement, should renounce important rights which the United States had always hitherto claimed in respect of the freedom of the seas is an indication of the wholly unrealistic course which it threatened to adopt – and this at a moment when prominent Europeans cherished feelings of respect for America, and regarded its power and strength as a 'last hope' if the day of reckoning should come.

71 Franklin Delano Roosevelt, the only president of the United States to have been elected to four terms of office. He is shown here in December 1941 making his first broadcast to a nation at war.

But the ship of state was still steered by Franklin D. Roosevelt. In his hands, the Neutrality Acts proved to be the pillars of the policy which he deemed it right to pursue. He took due note of the Abyssinian War, and the ban on arms deliveries hit Italy harder than Abyssinia (which it would, in any case, have been difficult to supply). Had the League of Nations remained true to its principles and persevered in its sanctions policy with US support, Italy might have found itself in a very tight corner. The Spanish Civil War provided an opportunity to overhaul and extend the Neutrality Acts. Increased powers were granted to the President. US arms deliveries were, after all, to be permitted in future, but with the cash-and-carry proviso that consignments must be paid for in cash and collected by the purchaser. Senator William Borah put his finger on the implications of this policy when, during a debate in March 1939, he declared, 'We seek to avoid all risks, all dangers, but we make certain to get all the profits.' The revision of American neutrality policy had begun with a campaign against the profit motive, and now the wheel had come full circle. The approach to the problem had, however, changed, as it later turned out.

During the Spanish Civil War the United States declined to join the non-intervention committee which had been sponsored by France, but the US administration pursued essentially the same political objectives. This evoked protests that the 'loyalists' were at a disadvantage because – contrary to official protestations – Franco's men were receiving aid and reinforcements from Hitler and Mussolini. However, the Spanish Republicans' links with the Soviet Union encouraged a policy of abstention in the United States as well as in Britain and France.

This exemplifies how the western powers increasingly abandoned the initiative to the dictator-states and adopted a policy of appeasement, an attitude which the militant powers inevitably regarded as an admission of defeat. As has been rightly observed, the western powers, including the United States, 'devitalized' each other; in other words, each looked to the other for weakness and submission.

PREPARATIONS FOR WAR

The political course had been set at the time of the Geneva Disarmament Conference (1932) and the London Economic Conference. Germany and Japan liquidated the 1919 peace settlement. The Versailles powers, France and Great Britain, failed to agree on a common policy towards Germany and were at odds with the United States on the subject of disarmament. Roosevelt continued to pursue his New Deal programme. By abstaining at the London conference he destroyed the possibility of effective collaboration with America's former allies in disarmament and defence policy. The French foreign minister of the time, Louis Barthou, saw greater promise in the development of relations with the East European countries of the Little Entente, and observed to the US delegate, Norman Davis, 'Sometimes the United States played a more active part when it was not present as a formal participant than when it was.'

Like his distant cousin Theodore at the beginning of the century, Franklin D. Roosevelt strove to gain support for the new orientation of his foreign policy in South America, christened the 'Good Neighbor' policy. It has already been mentioned in another guise, when we showed how Theodore Roosevelt extended the Monroe Doctrine, and gave it a new meaning. President Wilson also sought to adapt the Monroe Doctrine to the new situation during the disputes with Mexico, when he declared his readiness to accept the mediation 135 of the ABC powers (Argentina, Brazil, Chile) in a negotiated settlement with America's immediate neighbour. In the same spirit, Franklin D. Roosevelt and his Secretary of State, Cordell Hull, sought to lend concrete shape to the pan-American idea during the 1930s. At the Montevideo Conference (December 1933), agreement was reached on the principle that 'no State has a right to intervene in the internal or external affairs of another'. Roosevelt lived up to that idea when he embarked on the gradual dismantling of US protectorates in Central America and formally withdrew the Roosevelt Corollary of his predecessor.

From the time of Roosevelt's 'quarantine' speech at Chicago (1937) it was evident that the President was striving to secure a timely hearing for America's voice in face of the threat of a new world war. It is true that he suffered spells of discouragement. The feud between the hard-line isolationists and the existing or potential supporters of an active European policy was dangerous, in that it obscured real issues and revived old passions. Roosevelt himself had failed to deal with the legacy of Hoover's foreign policy, and, preoccupied with the New Deal, sacrificed an active European policy to his new domestic programme. He could, in fact, be accused of having personally smoothed the way for the new nationalism.

Just as Hoover regarded the events of 1914–18 as the starting-point of the Great Depression, Roosevelt maintained that rearmament in the 1930s was to blame for hindering a proper resumption of world trade. It is to Roosevelt's credit that, in Hull's reciprocal trade programme, his moves towards liberalizing trade compared favourably with the high-tariff policy of his Republican predecessors. Latin America also was included in the reciprocal trade programme, and American recognition of Soviet Russia in 1934 was likewise intended as a step towards the resumption of commercial relations. (It was even hoped that this would pave the way for a settlement of the debt question.)

Recent research into foreign policy during the New Deal era has made it plain that, by rigorously eschewing multilateral trade and the most-favoured-nation principle in favour of bilateral agreements (in the hope of securing particularly advantageous terms by an ostensible readiness to settle outstanding debts), Nazi Germany seriously disrupted US plans and considerably strengthened Roosevelt's determination to fight if necessary. The United States felt threatened by

German competition in the South American market, as elsewhere.

At the time of the Czech crisis, Roosevelt could be seen edging gradually towards a stand against the National Socialist policy of expansion and intervention. In September 1938 the President appealed to Hitler and Mussolini to resolve the Czech issue by peaceful negotiation. He thus helped to pave the way for the Munich Conference. Its outcome, the Munich Agreement, signified the abandonment of the policy put forward some years earlier by Barthou. Links with the east were loosened, as the Stalin-Ribbentrop pact was to prove. A more active Atlantic-oriented policy became the only possible alternative.

What happened at Munich dictated the key ideas of the Lima Declaration (December 1938), subscribed to by the delegates of twenty-one American republics. This confirmed that all members of the Pan-American Conference possessed the right of self-determination, but went on to record their concerted will to resist 'foreign intervention or activities that may threaten them'. The United States would have preferred to indicate even more clearly the quarter to which this warning was addressed.

The trade agreement signed with Great Britain in 1938, and the British royal couple's visit to Washington early in the following year (the first such visit in history), were belated signs of a *rapprochement* between the United States and its allies inaugurated at the time of the 1917–18 ordeal.

When Czechoslovakia was forced to submit to Hitler in spring 1939, Roosevelt sent letters to Hitler and Mussolini demanding to know if they contemplated similar action against thirty-one other nations which he listed by name. He also revived the subject of a disarmament conference. Meanwhile, at the beginning of the year, he had secured congressional approval of a first defence budget (roughly 500 million dollars) whose aim was to strengthen defences in the Pacific and Caribbean and expand the air force. The 'democracies' grew closer together when France was permitted to purchase aircraft in the United States. On 4 November 1939, two months after the outbreak of World War II, Congress annulled the chief provision of the Neutrality Acts: it lifted the arms embargo but retained the cash-and-carry principle.

The increasing military preparedness of the United States (after neutrality had been proclaimed on 5 September) is evidenced by 137

measures taken during the period up to the formal commencement
of hostilities on 8 December 1941. (The Japanese assault on Hawaii and
the Philippines came on 7 December 1941.) To enumerate these
briefly: at Panama on 2 October 1939 the Pan-American Conference
proclaimed the existence of a security zone extending round the continent to a distance of 300 miles from the coast, within which area no
acts of war would be tolerated. On 20 July 1940 the President signed a
law providing for a 'two-ocean navy' to protect the western hemisphere. On 16 May 1940 Congress passed a 2½-billion-dollar budget
for reinforcing the navy and army and set an annual production target
of 50,000 aircraft. In the same year, a start was made on the recruitment of 1,200,000 combat troops and 800,000 reserves. On 2 September 1940 the 'destroyer-base' deal between Churchill and

138

Roosevelt was concluded. Under this, the United States acquired leases on British naval and air stations extending from Newfoundland to British Guiana in exchange for the transfer to the Royal Navy of fifty (obsolete) destroyers.

The United States demonstrated its readiness to co-operate on a more active basis by passing the Lend-Lease Act of 11 March 1941, in which it stood revealed as the 'arsenal of the democracies' by proclaiming that it would supply arms (without claim to repayment but in return for certain concessions) to all countries which the President might deem it expedient to assist.

There were numerous other tokens that the United States was actively preparing to fight if need be. True to the spirit of the Monroe Declaration, it informed the governments of Europe that it would not recognize the transfer of possessions on the American continent from one European government to another (e.g. from the Netherlands to Germany). A system of forward bases was built up by the treaty with Denmark (10 April 1941) concerning the defence of Greenland, under which the United States was granted the right to construct naval and air bases there, and also by US acceptance of an invitation from the Icelandic government to relieve Britain by sending American troops to replace the British forces stationed there. The despatch of US forces to Surinam to protect industrial installations from the subversive attentions of Axis agents was intended to forestall a potential German take-over before it could assume tangible form. Finally, naval patrols were empowered – after a US destroyer had been engaged by a U-boat – not to wait until attacked in future but 'to strike their deadly blow first'.

Roosevelt did not know whether Hitler himself would swallow such a provocation. As it happened, Hitler's Japanese allies anticipated him by attacking Pearl Harbor and the Philippines. Congress duly declared war on Japan (8 December 1941); on 11 December 1941 Germany and Italy declared war on the United States. Wholly in keeping with the logic of history, the United States was challenged in the Pacific. Contrary to the logic of history, so it appeared, the President and his naval and military advisers decided that the war in Europe should take priority. This confirms one of the main arguments of the present study, namely, that expansionist policy in the Far West and the Pacific always prompted the United States to 'reinsure' in Europe, that America felt a need at moments of extreme 139 crisis to reactivate the spiritual reserves which it shared with Europe by first coming to Europe's aid. Goaded into war by Japan, it turned with even greater vehemence on Europe than on Asia, whence the attack had come.

Roosevelt would have found himself in an awkward predicament if Japan had overrun British, French and Dutch possessions in South-East Asia and threatened India without launching a direct assault on US territory. Japan had signalled the 'revolt of Asia' and the Asian challenge to the west in the Russo-Japanese War of 1904–5, a war which set off the chain reaction leading to World War I. Its second thrust, aimed this time at America but, by implication, at Europe as well, initiated yet another chapter in world history and gave to World War II an even more global character than the first. Japan also created for the first time a genuine 'western front' by thrusting America back on Europe. On the other hand, America's defeat of Japan helped Russia to revenge itself on the Japanese. The collapse of Japan's China front enabled the Chinese, with Russian support, to carry through the great revival which the United States would gladly have sponsored, but which now assumed a communist form. The Rome–Berlin–Tokyo Axis had called the existing world order in question; the answer was supplied by Russia and the United States.

73, 74 The beginning and the end. Left, the Japanese attack on Pearl
Harbor, 7 December 1941; above, the landing in France on D–day, 6 June
1944.

75 Atomic bomb explosion at Bikini Atoll, 25 July 1946 – supreme symbol of the United States as super-power.

IV   THE UNITED STATES, SUPER-POWER OF THE WEST

A NEW INTERNATIONAL CONFIGURATION

The development of relations between the United States and Europe from the outbreak of World War II to the present is of decisive importance. It is a period during which the fortunes of both have taken a surprising and unpredictable turn. Hitler so weakened the European concert of powers and its almost worldwide colonial system that it could not survive in its existing shape. Only the United States could fill the breach. It checked the collapse of Europe, took over from another base – the American continent – the hegemony which Western Europe had hitherto enjoyed, and exercised it with objectives which differed as widely from those of the European powers as the new political climate differed from the old.

The United States built itself the position of a super-power, and established what amounted, in Ernest R. May's phrase, to a 'free world empire'. The 'American Century' proved to be more than a propaganda slogan; the period from about the middle of the century to the present (1940–70) has clearly borne the stamp of US expansion and US influence, both of which have extended not only to Europe but to Asia and Africa and deep into the camp of the opposing super-power, the Soviet Union and its satellites.

The path which led to the free world empire of the United States was extremely involved. The initial phase (from 1939 to December 1941) was characterized by indirect involvement in World War II even before the United States became a full partner, the second phase by direct participation and the maintenance of an offensive on two fronts, Atlantic and Pacific, until the total overthrow of the two main hostile powers, Germany and Japan. There followed, concurrently with the establishment of the United Nations Organization, a phase of demobilization and military withdrawal from Europe, succeeded – before withdrawal was complete – by a continuation of the war in another form (no peace settlement having been concluded with Germany), namely, as a 'cold' war against the Soviet Union and   143 communist expansion and infiltration. This conflict still drags on. 'Hot' war is limited to certain extra-European trouble-spots where domestic political instability prevails. 'Cold' war occurs at focal points in the power-struggle between the United States and the Soviet Union. 'Peaceful coexistence' reigns in Europe and the world at large now that a 'balance of terror' has been established between the two super-powers.

During this thirty-year period the United States has undergone a strange experience. It started out in the hope and belief that it was eradicating an intolerable and despotic régime which signified a present and continuing threat to the whole of mankind. This goal accorded with traditional US policy because, ever since the Union's inauguration as a federal republic, Americans had seen the fight for freedom as their special assignment within the community of nations.

It is, of course, true that the United States decided to enter the war only when it was threatened in its own territory and territorial waters and when it became the victim of direct aggression. It joined forces with belligerents which had already been engaged in a merciless struggle for survival, Britain for more than two years and the Soviet Union for several months. The war was waged in coalition, even though no formal alliance was concluded between the USA and the USSR. After twenty-four other countries had joined them, Britain and the United States formally proclaimed that the war was being fought by the 'United Nations', of which Russia was one. Unlike 1918, the foundations of a new international pact were laid while the war was still in progress. Shortly after the capitulation of Hitler's Germany this pact was signed at San Francisco and a preliminary assembly, attended by representatives of fifty-one nations and presided over by the Belgian premier, Henri Spaak, was convened in January 1946. The United States now believed that it had eliminated the world's misfortunes and escaped the vicious circle.

The task which Woodrow Wilson had unsuccessfully tackled twenty-seven years earlier was now resumed. This time the signs were deemed to be more auspicious because the two major belligerent powers, the USA and the USSR, whose absence from the League of Nations had widely been regarded as its congenital defect, not only took part but were rated the pillars of the whole institution. The United States believed that the creation of UNO represented the definitive step from war to peace. The country prepared for a return

76 The siting of the United Nations headquarters in New York City could be interpreted as an indication of US determination to play a leading role in international affairs and to turn its back on the isolationism of the pre-war period.

to pre-war isolation. If crises arose there would be recourse to UNO, which had been installed on American soil. The Security Council and the General Assembly between them would steer problems towards a solution acceptable to all.

But things took a different course. America's basic political tenets reposed on ideas that hailed from an 'era of free security' which had just come to an end. Short-term planning for victory and the separation of military and political considerations engendered a belief

77 British cartoon (1945) of
the three wartime leaders
reconstituting the map of
Europe.

78 The Soviet sphere of
influence in Berlin indicated
by street signs.

that peace would be guaranteed by a form of US–Soviet condominium, within which Soviet Russia and the United States would enjoy
parallel spheres of influence: a system so constituted that Europe, too,
would effectively be divided into an eastern and a western zone. The
moral and political basis of the new order was furnished by the
principles of the Atlantic Charter as incorporated in the United
Nations pact. However, these were variously construed and interpreted by east and west. This emerged from the treatment of Poland,
for whose preservation the western powers had gone to war, and then
over the question of Germany. Differences arose, divergences
revealed themselves and conflicts materialized which caused the
war-time alliance to disintegrate.

It was as though the scales had fallen from American eyes. The
administration quickly caught up on the planning which had hitherto
been neglected. Now – for the first time – the United States seized the
initiative. In a unique change of policy, it threw off the armour of
isolationism and neutralism. Confirmed in its views by communist
146   action in Prague in 1948, which seemed to be modelled on that of

Adolf Hitler, the United States proclaimed its allegiance to the principle of wide-ranging, and ultimately global, intervention in the name of resistance to the communist menace and the containment of further communist expansion.

The Truman Doctrine (12 March 1947), a first step towards deliberate 'entanglement' across the Atlantic ('to help free peoples to maintain . . . their national integrity'); the speech by General Marshall, Truman's Secretary of State, at Harvard University (5 June 1947), calling for a European recovery programme; Truman's inaugural address after his election to the Presidency (20 January 1949), which contained as 'Point Four' a programme of comprehensive aid for underdeveloped countries; and, later, the 'Eisenhower Doctrine', aimed at preserving the independence of Middle Eastern countries which solicited US aid – all these were indications that the United States had changed course and set itself new objectives: that it had, in fact, abandoned a policy focused exclusively or even primarily on the American continent, in favour of one directed specifically at Europe but also at the entire world.

147

This approach went far beyond Wilsonism, which, although ideologically global, was manifestly based on the common self-interest of different peoples, who were supposed to thrash out their conflicts peacefully at the political level, just as they engaged in peaceful economic competition. Now, however, in the different doctrines mentioned above and the programmes and institutions based on them, the United States took the field like an imperial power, offering aid, funds, goods, arms and, eventually, troops and military assistance.

In this way the 'American Century' really materialized. In the twenty years that followed the Berlin blockade of 1948, the United States organized the NATO military pact in Europe, SEATO in Asia, ANZUS in the Pacific and CENTO in the Middle East, joined with Latin America in establishing the Organization of American States (OAS), and concluded more than fifty bilateral military agreements, with, for instance, Japan, the Philippines, several countries in South-East Asia, and the immediate neighbours of Russia in the Middle East. The whole system was sustained by economic aid in a wide variety of forms, ranging from voluntary contributions and gifts to interest-bearing loans or direct US business investment in highly industrialized countries, as well as in underdeveloped agricultural lands with rich resources of raw materials.

If one seeks for parallels, one thinks of British expansion in the nineteenth century, of the empire founded on British maritime, financial and commercial supremacy which opened up new worlds for European trade to conquer in Africa, Asia, North and South America and Australasia. One thinks back to late antiquity – a period when the American continent was still unknown – and the influence of the Roman Empire extending far into Asia.

However, the more obvious and meaningful comparison, because it is clearer and more easily appraised, is with America's great antagonist, the Soviet Union. The United States and the Soviet Union emerged as rivals for world supremacy after World War II. Both have, or lay claim to, a mission. Both operate in the twentieth-century age of progressive industrialization, of colonial emancipation, of the atomic and the hydrogen bomb. It is also the age of a new revolution, that of the Chinese, with which both super-powers are much preoccupied.

China was an American protégé of long standing. It was China which brought the United States into World War II, in so far as the

79 This cartoon from *Krokodil* shows the American G.I. putting festoons of rockets around a doubtful-looking Europe.

United States supported Chinese resistance to Japan, just as it had issued a clear warning to Japan in the Manchurian conflict as early as 1932.

The crucial turning-point in world politics was America's decision, after the attack of Pearl Harbor, not to give priority to the war in the Pacific, which would have accorded with US tradition, but to concentrate on the war in Europe against Hitler. This was tantamount to taking pressure off the Russians, who for their part declared at Yalta their readiness to enter the war against Japan (which had signed a neutrality pact with Russia in 1941). Although Hiroshima and Nagasaki rendered this step unnecessary, it gave the Russians the satisfaction of reversing the decision of 1904–5 in Manchuria.

149

While concentrating on Europe and contributing heavily to its military and economic recovery, the United States saw China escape from its sphere of influence. The People's Republic of China came into being with Soviet help and recognition, and the communists, who had been checked in the west by Western Europe's growing strength, resorted to military aggression in the east – in Korea. The result was a reversal of fronts. Europeans complained that the Americans were committing themselves in Asia instead of continuing to help Europe. The Korean War seemed to prove that the United States had no intention of abandoning its Far East policy for Europe's sake.

This benefited Europe in one respect, because it gave a fillip to those who wished to build a new Europe, not merely through American collaboration but rather by uniting the Europeans themselves. Soviet Russia was faced with a problem analogous to that which confronted the United States. China at first seemed a Russian protégé, an ally which would unlock the Asiatic world for communism. Feeling that pressure had been relieved in the east, Russia pursued its interests in Europe. Russian superiority became apparent during the Khrushchev era, and thus activated the defensive system which John Foster Dulles thought it necessary to erect as a bulwark against the expansionist pressure of the eastern powers.

With the loss of China, Europe acquired central importance as an American stronghold. Only after the outbreak of conflict between Soviet Russia and the Chinese People's Republic has a new situation come about. The phase of US-Soviet duopoly is drawing to an end. As it looks ahead at the 1970s, the United States aspires to 'disengagement' in foreign policy: American hopes are pinned on a strengthened Europe and a stronger Far East.

EAST-WEST ANTAGONISM

America's rise to super-power status was founded on its immense economic achievements. The war not only put an end to the depression of the 1930s but brought with it an unprecedented economic boom which spread from America to Europe after the conclusion of hostilities, and was taken up and developed by the Europeans themselves.

Thus, political and economic expansion went hand in hand. The United States experimented with economic aid, military support, credits and funding operations, consignments of goods; it despatched experts and set up a youth organization (the Peace Corps) for the benefit of underdeveloped countries, but it also sent armies, ploughed the oceans with its battle fleets and deployed the world's largest air force. Further development in the field of atomic weapons produced the hydrogen bomb.

The United States had found an adversary in Soviet Russia, and it was this antagonism which stimulated the development and cultivation of its own global power. Four variants or styles of US intervention, sometimes representing phases in a continuing process, are clearly visible and distinguishable: first, greater emphasis on economic aid than military; conversely, greater stress on military support than economic; next, parallel economic and military aid; and, last, exclusively military or exclusively economic backing.

Where the United States and Soviet Russia are concerned, the Cold War has been a story of mutual advances, mutual exhaustion, mutual friction. It has become a duel and contest in all fields of endeavour, particularly manifest in the space race, in the launching of earth satellites, and latterly in the race to reconnoitre and land on the moon. Already, unmanned probes have reached Venus and Mars.

80 The Peace Corps in action, an idealistic aspect of US global power.

81 An American painting ironically titled *Watch on the Rhine*, reflecting
US military presence in West Germany.

82 *Krokodil* cartoon at the time of Sputnik I (1957); the caption reads, 'Try looking down on them now.'

What really matters, however, is the contest in the armaments sector. In 1949 the Russians overhauled the Americans by developing an atomic weapon of their own and thus breaking the US world monopoly. The H-bomb put the Americans ahead once more, though not for long. Nothing humiliated the Americans more deeply than the lead which Russia gained in space by launching Sputnik I. The nuclear-powered submarine gave them a renewed lead, but one which the Russians soon wiped out. Stock-piling of atomic weapons is the main factor in stabilizing relations between the two countries, but it also shows every sign of becoming an umbrella beneath which smaller allies can fight their protectors' battle for them, with adverse reactions on the relations between the two principals.

Underlying this whole process is a basic revolutionary trend that should not be overlooked. It marks the dawn of a new era. The twentieth century began to reveal its true character with the Russian Revolution. Under fascism and National Socialism, state bureaucracy acquired a new significance *vis-à-vis* society and the economy. Whereas the old liberal order insisted on keeping government and economy separate, the world economic crisis proved insoluble, even in capitalist countries, without government intervention. The war was a triumph for state control, and made it extremely difficult for the United States to return to 'normalcy'. This is where the renewal of the whole fabric of social life throughout the entire world is being revolutionized.

It was by being sucked into the vortex of major international conflicts that the United States first assumed the dimensions of a genuine world power. Confrontation with Russia, which it at first sought to avoid, but later boldly accepted – many would say provoked or intensified – brought it face to face with the question of its mission and identity in the new era of mass civilization and global interdependence. The viability of the capitalist system was at stake. Was America a match for the socialist world and the empire of the people's democracies?

All the public actions of every US president of the period have sought to answer this question affirmatively. The dominant American idea is that the United States should be prepared to give help wherever there exists a firm desire for deliverance from chaos or communist tyranny. Peoples that have gained their independence shall be assisted to retain it; peoples that are still unemancipated shall be helped to gain their freedom. In this field too, Soviet Russia and the United States have become rivals, for what do the Soviet leaders offer prospective clients if not deliverance from the yoke of colonial domination?

Under fire from the Soviet Union, the 'American system' is acquiring quite novel characteristics, but ones always borrowed from the American past. There is talk of global isolationism, of the United States turning itself into a 'world policeman' (an expression whose negative connotation, in the sense of standing outside the fray, has become officially recognized since President Nixon took office). The fact of US military strength is new, of course. Its symbol is the Pentagon, the seat of the military administration. Its outward expression is a defence budget in the region of 80 billion dollars (40 per cent of total expenditure in 1969) and the ever-present fact of worldwide commitments. The purpose of US policy could only be to offer an alternative to communism. President Truman was obviously aiming at this in his 1949 inaugural address, when he asserted in Point Four that it was the task and duty of prosperous nations to assist those that were weak and impoverished.

83 A painting, from the United States Air Force Art Collection, called *Return for a Reload*, commemorating the Berlin Airlift in 1949.

The American people have fulfilled this task. They began by resisting the humiliation of the Berlin blockade and simultaneously offering generous economic aid in the interest of European recovery. The United States then declared its readiness to assist in establishing a line of defence by contributing military forces to a European army still in the process of creation. In pursuing this policy towards Europe, it adopted an entirely new line of political and economic thought: economic recovery as a prerequisite of the capacity for political action. This, indeed, had been the intention of Point Four – to evolve a new form of 'colonial policy' in the hope of winning the allegiance of the Third World.

Has America benefited from its endeavours? Has the world recognized its achievements for what they are? Our answer depends on whether we feel that we have been given a better world to live in.

Countries on good terms with the United States have never fared better economically, judging by their rise in living standards, and the Americans have successfully – if thanklessly – played the role of world policeman.

For the United States, it has been a trying period. The Berlin crisis had not long subsided when Korea flared up – a war which lasted for three years and cost the lives of more than 50,000 US soldiers. No less than 100,000 were wounded. When the French liquidated their colonial empires in Indo-China and Algeria, the United States – after hesitating to come to France's aid – took over its former role in Indo-China by helping to erect the provisional state of South Vietnam as a bulwark against the Vietminh. Despite armistice talks and a reduced military involvement, the United States has still to extricate itself from the war in Vietnam.

The United States tolerated the rise of a communist régime in Cuba. After the ill-fated 'Bay of Pigs' incident (1961), it played a waiting game until the Russians decided to withdraw from Cuba when the island was publicly 'quarantined' by President Kennedy, in response to the Russian build-up of missiles.

The gravest crisis of the post-war era was the Suez war of 1956, the effects of which are still perceptible today. This taught 'Atlantic-minded' Europeans that the NATO alliance cannot imply a one-sided attachment to Europe by the United States. It signified for both a claim to a greater margin of freedom to manœuvre, and ultimately paved the way for clarification and *rapprochement* on a new basis.

84 Action in the Korean War, in which the United States sought to stem
the power of communism in the Far East.

The Suez crisis arose because the United States formed a truly
global assessment of a regional situation. By abstaining from the Suez
adventure, it introduced itself to the world – after the military fiasco
of the western powers – as Europe's successor. In announcing his
promise of aid to the countries of the Middle East in the following
year, Eisenhower followed in the footsteps of the old European
Levantine powers. The intervention of US troops in the Lebanon
(1958) demonstrated America's presence. In this way, it continued to
pursue a policy which represented an alternative to communism.

Towards the end of the 1960s, polycentrism created a new situation.
The consolidation of the Chinese People's Republic, on the one hand, 159

and of the European Economic Community, on the other, has presented the two super-powers with new problems. The Soviet Union, which sees itself heavily committed in the east once more, is seeking security in the west by trying to preserve and reinforce the *status quo*. The United States is acquiring greater scope for manœuvre in Europe, because its position in Europe is built into the *status quo* (the Four-Power Statute relating to Germany) and its right of participation guaranteed. At the same time, a China recalcitrant towards the Soviet Union may eventually help the United States in normalizing its policy of non-recognition of the People's Republic. Now that the focus of the power-struggle has so patently shifted to Asia, where the United States is committed in its role as a Pacific power, the remoulding of relations with Japan will become the most delicate problem confronting those responsible for US foreign policy.

World War II, which revolved round the problem of Germany and Japan, continues to smoulder, but in another form. In Europe the outstanding issue is still that of Germany, but West Germany has become America's most trusted ally; in the Far East it is Japan, which is also closely linked with America. 'Europe or Asia first?' is a question which opens up new political perspectives. Viewed from this angle, the relationship between the United States and Europe that has grown out of World War II and the post-war period acquires fundamental importance. Is it conceivable that, given the existence of NATO and the close ties between the powers of the Atlantic area, the west could again exert a decisive influence on the course of the struggle for Asia and the Third World?

In an age of revolutionary changes, it was really the war and the post-war period that first transformed the transatlantic relationship into a historically relevant problem. That it did so was due principally to American initiative.

Europe moved to the centre of the stage under the impact of Axis plans for a new world order. It was not without significance that Roosevelt's policy was founded on the traditional ties with Britain. It was still more significant that, in the person of Winston Churchill, who was half-American himself and conducted the celebrated correspondence with Roosevelt under the pseudonym 'former naval person' (a reference to his Admiralty connections in World War I), Britain acquired a leader who differed from Chamberlain in attaching great importance to American sympathy and political backing.

85 The famous meeting of Churchill, Roosevelt and Stalin at Yalta in February 1945.

Having jolted his fellow-countrymen into a new mood with the New Deal, reminded them of the pioneering ideals of earlier days after the *belle époque* of the 1920s, and introduced them to European ideas of social reform, Roosevelt felt impelled – as his Chicago speech showed – to lead the United States out of its isolationism. It is true that Congress resisted this move with its Neutrality Acts, which tended in precisely the opposite direction, but Roosevelt spoke out on two occasions, once at the time of the Munich Conference and again during the Polish crisis of 1939. By so doing, he let Europeans know that the United States was an interested observer of the events that were unfolding in Europe.

In the Pacific, Prince Fumumaro Konoye, the Japanese premier, proclaimed a new order in Asia; this was a thrust in the same direction as Hitler's in Europe – in other words, it aimed at the overthrow of the existing power structure. The United States responded to 161

Japan's action in 1940 by terminating the 1911 trade agreement with Japan. The conclusion of the three-power pact between Germany, Italy and Japan on 27 September 1940 confirmed the new political orientation, for which the ground had been prepared by the Anti-Comintern Pact of 1936.

The counter-offensive of the democracies took shape from that moment onwards. Roosevelt was just the man to recognize America's hour of destiny and, when war broke out in December 1941, to work out plans for a global counter-attack from the incomparable base which the American continent afforded. Thanks to America's arsenal of weapons, ships, aircraft and – that grisly masterpiece – the atom bomb, the anti-Axis powers and the Soviet Union together won the war, and attained the preordained goal of unconditional surrender, in other words, of total victory in Europe and Asia.

We have already noted that the United States was favoured by the 'staggering' of events – or disasters – from 1938 onwards, in that it could initially assume the role of an 'arsenal of democracy' and supply arms to the western powers, and then, having itself become a belligerent, enter the lists with some degree of military preparedness. It should be added that, in contrast with its practice in World War I, it treated its allies in a financially generous manner under the terms of the Lend-Lease system.

Working in close harness with the British, the Americans increasingly assumed effective leadership, militarily, strategically and politically. It was inevitable that American ideas should acquire increasing weight and that Roosevelt should impose his point of view on Churchill. This became glaringly obvious over the question of the second front, after Churchill had earlier managed to secure US participation in the North African and Italian campaigns. The Americans pinned all their hopes on a direct thrust at Germany across the Channel, an operation in which they wanted all available forces to be used. The Russians were bearing down on Central Europe from the east, and it was the duty of the western powers to support them by attacking from the west. In the Pacific, the Americans were gradually working their way forward towards the Japanese islands from the south and east. Like Napoleon, Hitler had planned a break-through into the Middle East, via North Africa and the Caucasus. After clearing the Italians out of East Africa, the British had waged a counter-offensive first in the Libyan desert, and then, in concert with the

Americans, from Morocco, which was to all intents and purposes won by British forces.

Churchill wanted to continue this campaign in Italy and build up a Balkan front so as to roll back the Germans from the south-east. He gained no support for this plan from the Americans, who preferred to reserve their main forces for the western front and were already contributing inadequate forces to the Italian campaign. The decision was of historic importance: the Americans left the Russians a free hand throughout Eastern Europe (effectively as far as the Adriatic), thereby prejudicing post-war policy. They had no understanding of the British position in the Mediterranean and Middle East at this juncture. On the other hand, it was clear that no outlay of armed force could be too great for the implementation of Operation Overlord, the cross-Channel thrust which would, it was hoped, decide the outcome of the war. The concentration of man and resources on this operation proved to be well advised: it brought victory, exactly as envisaged in the strategy agreed with Stalin.

It was another question when it came to planning a peace settlement. In particular, doubt and uncertainty reigned in regard to the treatment of Germany, hence the setting-up of a four-power government which included – at Roosevelt's suggestion – the French. As to Eastern Europe, the Soviet Union and the United States each placed its own interpretation on the principles agreed at Yalta for the peace settlement there, which were supposed to harmonize with the spirit of the Atlantic Charter. But the former was in military control and had no difficulty in building up a forward line of communist satellite states where the Versailles powers had once installed a *cordon sanitaire* between Central Europe and the Soviet Union.

As for Germany, each member of the war-time alliance cherished a different idea: the British hoped for a federation oriented more towards the states of Southern Germany than towards Prussia; the Russians, a centralized state run on lines agreeable to the Soviet Union. The Americans vacillated; at first they proposed an economically weak structure which could never again disturb the peace, but later they advocated a 'democratic Germany' which was destined to become the very cornerstone of a new European system.

The establishment of an effective American foothold in Europe imparted a new twist to the centuries-old transatlantic relationship, and was of profoundest importance. It was in no respect premeditated 163 or intentional, and was in many ways the biggest surprise of the post-war period. The general belief, which Roosevelt shared, was that the US forces could be withdrawn within two years of the cessation of hostilities. The continuing American presence therefore represented a fundamental shift in international relations, and formed part of the international displacements and internal economic and social upheavals which the twentieth century has brought in its train.

THE SOVIET SHADOW

No broad view of this development is possible unless we divide the process into phases and single out individual features for emphasis before attempting a general assessment. A number of important points must, however, be mentioned immediately.

Hitler had succeeded in destroying Europe by posing as its re-generator. Because his Europe presupposed the overthrow of Soviet Russia and instead Stalin threw back the German armies and advanced into Central Europe, almost a millennium of German expansion eastwards was transformed into Russian expansion westwards and a total withdrawal of the German population from the eastern terri-tories. From 1945 onwards, the shadow of Russia lay across Europe. As the war drew to an end an 'east wind' blew in the German-occupied territories of Western Europe. There was a pro-Soviet orientation in the communist-permeated resistance movements, which had not only eroded Nazi control by waging guerrilla warfare, but had also drawn up plans for the building of a new Europe now that the old was bankrupt.

The communists were determined to take a hand in fashioning this future. Victorious Russia seemed to be living proof that the Soviet state represented a valid alternative to 'fascist' Europe. It had, after all, proved strong enough to resist Hitler and compel him to retreat, and Hitler had failed to induce the Russian people to desert Stalin.

Victory in World War II put Soviet Russia in a very strong position with regard to any disputes which arose about the formation of a new Europe. What was more, a certain understanding grew up between Roosevelt and Stalin, particularly towards the end of the war, in con-nection with Roosevelt's desire that the Soviet Union should par-ticipate in the defeat of Japan.

But at this very moment American success in atomic fission and the use of the A-bomb, which swiftly brought about Japan's surrender, created a new situation. Russia's contribution had proved to be superfluous, but the Soviet Union lost no opportunity to reactivate its Far East policy and to establish a new basis for co-operation with the Chinese communists in Manchuria. In turn, the United States did not invite the Soviet Union to the peace talks with the Japanese at San Francisco in 1951, and thus proclaimed that it regarded the defeat of Japan as its own single-handed achievement.

The years between 1945 and 1951 were characterized by two elemental series of events which took place on Russia's western and eastern flanks – in Western Europe and China. What was at stake in both cases was, in the last analysis, decisive communist infiltration of the western world. In Western Europe, powerful communist parties strove for a dominant position in the newly established post-war governments – particularly in France and Italy – but failed to gain control. In Great Britain, Churchill's party was heavily defeated by Labour in 1945. Attlee took over the reins of government and succeeded Churchill halfway through the Potsdam Conference. Socialist parties also came to power elsewhere in Europe (Holland, Scandinavia), but this signified the opposite of revolution and overthrow. Instead, the socialists made it their business, during the post-war boom, to spread prosperity among the lower orders of society, and thus became increasingly middle class in outlook, and even the champions of a reviving nationalism.

The intention was to conclude the war by a peace conference (which met at Paris in 1945 and 1946). Peace treaties were duly signed with Italy, Bulgaria, Rumania, Hungary and Finland (10 February 1947). No peace treaty was concluded with Germany, although the victorious powers had pledged themselves to this at Potsdam. Germany, the author of nearly six years of global conflict, became even in defeat the chief problem of the post-war era and a bone of contention between the victors.

The Soviet Union's post-war problems were immense. By virtue of the Russian advance into Central Europe, Stalin was able to install communist or pro-Russian governments in the Soviet-occupied territories. Above all, he intended the new Germany to come under Russian influence.

Exasperated by the treatment of Poland, which contravened the Yalta agreements, provoked by communist ventures in Greece and northern Iran, and alerted by Churchill's Fulton speech in March 1946   165

86 'Make way for the Marshall Plan', a German poster.

about the 'iron curtain' that now extended from Stettin to Trieste, the United States was overcome by that same feeling which Roosevelt had voiced at Chicago in 1937, when Hitler's geopolitical plans were beginning to take palpable shape: namely, that the world was threatened by a totalitarian régime which must be opposed. There was also a secret vow whose burden was 'never again'. Such was the spirit personified by Harry S. Truman, lower-middle-class successor of the urbane and cosmopolitan Roosevelt. Once he had overcome his initial uncertainties in the sphere of international relations, Truman found his feet and realized that fate had assigned America the role hitherto played by Europe.

On the eastern flank of the Eurasian continent a new China came into being – the Chinese People's Republic. While the United States was still debating whether or not to recognize the new state, the Korean War broke out – a war which could only be construed as a Soviet attempt to aggravate the conflict in Western Europe by an attack on one of the few remaining non-communist territories on the mainland of East Asia, South Korea. This transformed a political controversy into a war and created an immense stir in the United States. McCarthyism was rampant, and bitter attacks and accusations of treason were levelled against anyone suspected of pro-Soviet or pro-Chinese sympathies. This was understandable, in so far as the whole conception of working in harness with Soviet Russia stood revealed as an illusion. The US government, it appeared, had failed to appreciate the danger of communist stratagems, and the American people suffered an enduring trauma.

It was at this very period that Russia succeeded in developing an atom bomb. The United States, which had relied on its monopoly of nuclear power to keep the Russians at bay, and which had been able to withdraw its troops rapidly from Europe after the end of the war because of its possession of this weapon, now had to engage in a renewed and progressive arms race with the Soviet Union.

Europe, on the other hand, alarmed by events in the Far East, concentrated its attention upon itself. It was the chief beneficiary of the Truman Doctrine and the Marshall Plan, which offered it the prospect of rapid economic recovery, and Americans were always telling it that it must tread the path of unity if it ever again wished to count as a power factor. This hint was extremely welcome to advocates of European union.

Since that time we have seen a series of military alliances and economic unions, succeeding, supplementing and superseding each other until we now have a sum of mutually complementary but also mutually competitive and opposing groups, which operate sometimes as integrating and sometimes as disintegrating factors. The goal envisaged by the United States of America was a United States of Europe destined to become its partner in a world of highly and less highly industrialized nations.

Two main tendencies are apparent. British initiative in 1947 led to the Treaty of Dunkirk, a military alliance which was expanded by the Brussels Five-Power Treaty of 1948. In 1949 the United States offered the signatories of the Brussels pact military assistance as their ally under the North Atlantic treaty. The Truman Doctrine and Marshall Plan were thus supplemented by a military alliance with Western Europe. Europe, now on the road to economic recovery, was prompted by American encouragement to embark on a programme of self-defence and economic self-help. This became apparent when 167

plans were drawn up in 1952 for a European Defence Community (EDC) and the first steps taken to form the Coal and Steel Community.

In the dispute which ensued over German participation in the EDC, the American government sponsored and encouraged the establishment of an independent German federal republic. It was also instrumental, after France's rejection of the EDC, in seeing that Germany joined the Brussels powers and was admitted to NATO (1955). Meanwhile, the Europeans had not only set up the Council of Europe with headquarters at Strasbourg (1949) but were expanding their Coal and Steel Community into the European Economic Community (EEC).

The United States also ensured that the administrative nucleus of an Atlantic partnership was retained. OEEC (Organization for European Economic Co-operation), created under the Marshall Plan, was converted into OECD (Organization for Economic Co-operation and Development), of which the United States and Canada became full members. Thus, parallel to NATO, an Atlantic economic group was established for the expansion of world trade and the co-ordination of western aid to underdeveloped countries (1960). The work of the EPU (European Payments Union) was crowned with success by the European monetary agreement, and the European members found their way back to convertibility. This facilitated the 1957 negotiations which led to the Treaty of Rome.

Great Britain, which maintained close military and political links with the United States, looked with some suspicion on the EEC, which it feared might infringe on its worldwide interests. When eventually it changed its attitude and applied for membership, it failed to gain admission. In the 1960s President de Gaulle twice pronounced British membership to be undesirable. Only after de Gaulle's resignation was it possible to reopen negotiations which this time were successful, though a majority of the British people was opposed to entry. But, France, which possessed no 'special relationship' with the United States, suffered a far more dramatic decline – in Indo-China and Algeria – in its status as a world power, until finally in 1958 it recalled de Gaulle, the heroic personification of French resistance, and sought to regain some of its past glory by building up a strong position in Europe. But it was the German Federal Republic, the cornerstone of the American system of alliances in the west, upon which the US relied to underpin its relationship with Europe.

169

87 The launching in the United States on 9 November 1967 of Saturn V.

In the long run, no doubt, a regenerated and economically thriving Europe could eventually become a renewed danger to the United States. This, however, was not evident at the time. The safeguard was that the new Europe was, in part at least, reconstituted by and economically linked with the United States, and in any case conflict with Russia and China made it imperative, in American eyes, that the 'west' should unite rather than divide.

THE TRUMAN AND EISENHOWER ERAS

In the turbulent post-war period, during which the whole shape of world politics was transformed, three countries have accelerated the course of development and left their mark on it: the Soviet Union, which pushed forward into Central Europe and sought to reinforce its position in the Far East by fostering the spread of communism; China, which Mao Tse-tung ranged among the world's major revolutionary powers; and the United States, which assumed responsibility for countering communist expansion and established itself as the dominant world power.

Relations between Europe and the United States since the beginning of World War II have none the less passed through a number of phases of attraction and revulsion. It was clear in the first place that it was impossible to win the war against Hitler without the United States. What was more, the United States was essential to the consolidation of that hard-won victory. The Americans were 'needed' in those days, and people were ready to fling themselves into their arms. For its part, the United States felt called upon to make a basic change in its policy – indeed, in the fundamental political maxims of neutralism and Americanism. This was the hopeful era; there were visions of supra-national European authorities – even of transatlantic super-authorities – which would transcend the antagonisms that existed between individual countries. Then came Korea and the sobering realization by Europeans that the United States was not exclusively concerned with Europe; while Americans, for their part, perceived in the post-1958 years that a healthy and prosperous Europe no longer had to follow the American lead but was capable of going its own way.

In this way a mood of disenchantment spread throughout the world. Its most eloquent expression was the Chinese cultural revolution, though there were cultural revolutions everywhere, in the sense
170 that the national idea and the national interest were once again put in

the forefront. As Harold van Cleveland has rightly observed, disillusion was understandable when one measures the realities of the 1960s against the great plans and expectations of the late 1940s and early 1950s.

What made it hard for the United States was that it took over Europe's role in the great-power conflict without having a 'European assignment', in other words, without having absorbed the political experience of Europe – not unnaturally, since it had rejected Europe's claim to leadership for a century and a half, and had ignored its achievements in this respect. The Soviet Union was trundling along the well-worn track left by traditional Tsarist expansionism. The Chinese People's Republic took it upon itself to transplant the heritage of Chinese imperial power into the world of today. The United States, an anti-world to all that has constituted history so far, found itself enmeshed in the history it rejected, and faced the impossible task of bearing, as it were, two thousand years of history in mind if it was to do justice to the tasks that fell to it. Europe, in turn, saw itself so buoyed up and sustained by American economic strength that it now began, with transatlantic brashness, to teach the Americans a lesson. Europeans blushed during the 1930s at their own submission to political blackmail by the dictatorships, whereas the 1960s saw them trying to persuade the Americans that they should back down and show some common sense!

There are three clearly discernible phases in the course of political developments between 1945 and 1970.

In the first phase, American-Soviet rivalry and conflict led to the establishment of a western front by the powers which opposed communist influence. The civil war in Greece and the British government's inability to intervene as a result of its financial weakness forced President Truman to take the initiative and proclaim that the United States would step in and help. The west received a 'face-lift' in the years between 1947 and 1952. The unification of the west took place against the backcloth of the first Berlin crisis. When the Russians attempted to isolate Berlin and make it ripe for surrender, the western powers countered not by sending ground troops to the city's approaches – which could have meant war – but by mounting an airlift, in which the RAF played a notable part, which kept Berlin alive for almost a year. The build-up of a network of US air bases in Europe, primarily in Great Britain, was a corollary of this.

171

The grand design of parallel economic and military reorganization assumed concrete form in bodies such as the WEU, OEEC, the Coal and Steel Community, and NATO. By concluding the EDC agreement, Europe sought to acquire its own forms of military organization on a multi-national basis. Controversy over the European Defence Community in the period 1952–54 gave a first inkling of the difficulties and problems that would attend the task of reconstruction. The British were not prepared to commit themselves militarily on the continent to a greater extent than their NATO obligations prescribed; in other words, not more so than the United States. The French ultimately rejected the whole framework of the treaty because they disliked the new policy of German participation and re-militarization.

We now come to the second phase, the years 1953–61, which opened with the end of the Truman administration and encompassed the Eisenhower and Dulles era. The 1950s stand in strong contrast to the preceding period. Stalin died in 1953, and Khrushchev asserted his political leadership with increasing force until 1958. Churchill, still at the head of the Conservative Party, reassumed the premiership of Great Britain in 1951. In France, de Gaulle was to come to power in 1958 and steer the Fifth Republic towards a national revival. More fundamentally, the years between 1953 and 1961 were a time of further vigorous reconstruction. Thanks to Franco-German understanding, which de Gaulle did his best to reinforce, the steps taken at the Messina conference in 1955 to form a west European economic community were crowned with success. With the signature of the Rome treaties (1957) and the establishment of the EEC (the 'Six') a league of states was set up in Western Europe which was animated by the vision of a new united Europe. It was counter-balanced in Central and Eastern Europe by a parallel economic organization of the communist states ('Comecon') and in the west by a grouping of countries (EFTA, the 'Seven'), of which Britain was the strongest constituent, with co-ordinated trade policies, created with a view to maintaining the worldwide commercial links which, it was believed, even a European organization should not surrender.

But the same period was also darkened by the shadows of failure, which were to grow still darker in the 1960s. True, Eisenhower was able to fulfil his pledge to end the Korean War, but it was by compromise rather than victory, and left a bitter taste in the mouths of many Americans. Meanwhile, the Russians had possessed the atom bomb from 1949 onwards, and in 1957 sent their first sputnik into space. Radical changes were taking place in the Soviet domain under the slogan of de-Stalinization. The satellite states scented the winds of change, and revolt and discontent became widespread; in 1956 there were uprisings in Poland and Hungary, while President Tito of Jugoslavia had withdrawn from the Cominform as early as 1948. Change also made itself felt in the 'third world' in a way not always comfortable for American interests. Egypt threw off its monarchical government in 1952 and Colonel Nasser constructed a personal régime of pan-Arab complexion. India, too, went its own way, independent of the great alliances.

It was into this world that Khrushchev tossed the slogan 'co-existence'. The United States, with John Foster Dulles in charge of foreign policy, at first responded by stepping up its counter-measures. Under Truman, George Kennan had formulated a policy of 'containment' as most suited to deal with the Russian challenge. Dulles, by contrast, called for a crusade against communist tyranny, and announced that the Soviet bloc and the United States were engaged in a power-struggle which had its roots in divergent political and ethical systems.

US-Soviet antagonism became so acute that Dulles spoke in terms of 'brinkmanship' and recommended 'massive retaliation' – i.e. nuclear warfare – as an instrument of policy. Under a veneer of summit conferences and tête-à-tête talks between world leaders (e.g. Eisenhower and Khrushchev at Camp David in September 1959) tension built up immeasurably during the 1950s, and acquired a new dimension as the space race began to assume distinct outlines. Dulles ringed the Soviet bloc with alliances and bases. SEATO (1954) was intended as an Asian counterpart of NATO, with functions in the Pacific area which corresponded to those of NATO in the Atlantic. In addition, there were a number of supplementary treaties, both multilateral and bilateral, whose effect was to make the United States seem the cornerstone of a military organization resembling, as we have already said, an informal empire – in which, however, the imperial power enjoyed no visible privileges. This structure was still opposed by a united communist bloc. Since 1950 China had been associated with Soviet Russia in a pact of mutual assistance which was intended to smooth China's path to industrialization, and, in the west, 173 the Soviet Union had in 1955 banded its allies and satellites together in the Warsaw Pact.

The Russians definitely held the initiative in Khrushchev's day. The domestic reforms he put through at the Twentieth Party Congress and after were very considerable, but they hardly entitle one to speak of a 'thaw' in Soviet foreign policy or accuse Dulles of nursing vindictive designs. Khrushchev provoked a new Berlin crisis (1958), an attempt to test the stability of the situation in Central Europe and counteract the impression of American success left by the founding of the German Federal Republic, its admission to the WEU and later to NATO, and the German 'economic miracle'.

All efforts to solve the German problem by establishing a 'neutral' demilitarized zone in Central Europe, in which the British, including Churchill himself, took the lead, came to nothing, though in America they enjoyed the support of George Kennan, the former leading State Department expert, and in Eastern Europe had the backing of the Poles, who put forward a variant of their own, the so-called Rapacki Plan. The conferences of Berlin (1954, at foreign-minister level) and Geneva (1955, a summit conference attended by Eisenhower, Bul-

ganin, Eden and Faure) were a fiasco. The Paris summit conference arranged for 1960 was cancelled by Khrushchev at the last moment, his pretext being the U-2 affair (violation of Soviet air space by a US reconnaissance plane). Eisenhower's refusal of an invitation to Russia and the cancellation of his Tokyo trip (abandoned for reasons of personal security) were symptomatic of a worsening situation.

In 1955, even before the Geneva Conference in July, Khrushchev had advocated a two-state system for Germany; in other words, he asserted that reunification could be effected only by means of an understanding between two sovereign German states. This set the course which, with the building of the Berlin Wall in 1961, not only split Germany into two parts but gave it two mutually opposing political systems. A similar tendency to division was implicit in the manœuvres of President de Gaulle, when he opposed a link-up between the Six and the Seven. Britain, which had requested admission to the Six under Macmillan's Conservative government, was turned down after negotiations which lasted from 1961 to 1963, and a further application by the Labour government several years later in 1967 met with the same fate.

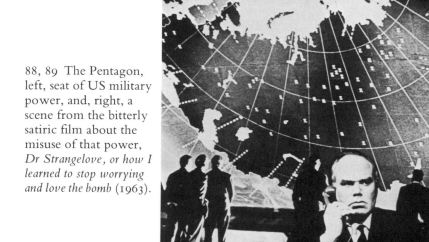

88, 89 The Pentagon, left, seat of US military power, and, right, a scene from the bitterly satiric film about the misuse of that power, *Dr Strangelove, or how I learned to stop worrying and love the bomb* (1963).

The economic strengthening of Europe had been initiated by the United States, and the plans of Monnet and Schuman and the Rome treaties were hailed with enthusiasm in some quarters in America. Then, its self-confidence restored, Western Europe indulged in the Suez adventure of 1956. Dulles, who had not been informed, left his maladroit allies in the lurch. Together with the USSR, he sponsored a UN resolution which placed the Canal Zone under the protection of a UN contingent. The Hungarian crisis occurred at the same period. Khrushchev threatened the west with massive retaliation, and Hungary's cries for help went unanswered. The Russians even refused to allow the UN Secretary-General to set foot on Hungarian soil. The United States, respecting the Soviet sphere of influence, stood back.

The Suez crisis exposed the dubious or ambivalent nature of the whole post-war establishment. Even after its remarkable revival, Europe was no longer the Europe of old. In Hungary and Egypt, the new super-powers had acted with an eye to their own (and mutual) interests. In 1957 the United States demonstrated by means of the Eisenhower Doctrine that it intended to act as successor to the western powers in the Near East, and showed that it was in earnest by intervening in the Lebanon. At the same time, Europe was moving towards the EEC, which became a reality in 1957.

De Gaulle's rejection of British membership of the EEC in 1963 was indirectly aimed at the United States, because the latter, which had consistently backed the 'Six', not the 'Seven', had favoured British entry. Having wound up its existing colonial policy and made peace with Algeria in 1962, France was trying to pursue a policy of regeneration of her own – one which ignored the United States – on the grounds that Europe had completed its recovery, and thus stood in no further need of US support. The old pre-war policy of the Third Republic and the tradition of French *gloire* were associated factors which contributed to an attempt at *rapprochement* with Russia.

FROM KENNEDY TO NIXON

The third phase of the post-war period coincides with Kennedy's administration in the United States, the Labour victory of 1964 in Britain, and the fall of Khrushchev in the Soviet Union. The new attitudes adopted by the United States were as much in conflict with the foreign policy pursued by Dulles as the road taken by Soviet Russia differed from the one it had followed under Khrushchev.

90 French President Charles de Gaulle, shown here during a visit of President John Kennedy to Paris in 1961, made a strong challenge to US hegemony over Western Europe.

The real key-note of the new phase of the mid- and late 1960s, was de Gaulle's decision to withdraw French forces completely from NATO command and remove all NATO installations from France (including USAF bases on French soil), without withdrawing from the NATO alliance itself, something which might still have been possible in 1959. The other principal factor was the growing dissension between Soviet Russia and Mao Tse-tung's China.

The 1960s were a time when fronts hardened and signs of fatigue became apparent, but also when glimmers of light appeared too. By the beginning of the 1970s a realization was growing on all sides that things could not be allowed to continue in the same old way. From the point of view of relations between the United States and Europe, the 1960s were a period when the consequences of US influence and participation became clearly apparent.

The United States exerted a massive influence on European thought and sentiments. In particular, pro-Americanism and anti-Americanism played a great part in shaping and strengthening the political conscience of Europeans. Many of the reactions were purely superficial, nor did public opinion follow a geographical pattern: there was more anti-Americanism in America than in many parts of Europe, and more enthusiasm for Europe among Americans than among many Europeans.

John F. Kennedy took an abrupt step into a new era. He strove to invest America's mission with fresh dignity and impact. NATO was allotted a new role in Kennedy's 'grand design': Europe was not to be a US satellite but a colleague in tackling the problems posed by the unequal development of rich nations and poor. Under Kennedy, the vision of an American alternative to the communist gospel took shape. It was not intended as a challenge to Soviet Russia. Instead, Kennedy and Khrushchev established contact and sought to take each other's measure. Kennedy's message was global and his watchword was 'interdependence'. In the military sphere he looked for a strategy which would avert nuclear war, and worked towards the limitation of armaments; in the economic sphere his goal was the promotion of world trade; in space travel his target was to overhaul the Russians within a decade. In fact the Americans reached the moon in the summer of 1969, almost at the same time as an unmanned Russian space-craft crashed to the surface not far from the American landing-place.

The Americans took the initiative in two respects during the 1960s, each time as a means of lending substance to their programme. Kennedy's Alliance for Progress was more a symbol than a genuine remedy for the neglect of Latin America in terms of international economic aid. By passing the Trade Expansion Act, Congress underpinned Kennedy's appeal for a general reduction of tariffs, which found expression in the Kennedy Round. The Geneva conference organized by the GATT (General Agreement on Tariffs and Trade) partners effected a general liberalization of trade through the lowering of tariffs (1964–67), while the special requirements of the developing countries were to be catered for at a meeting of the United Nations Conference on Trade and Development (UNCTAD).

The second major achievement of the Kennedy administration was to stabilize relations with Soviet Russia. This success resulted from a political gamble whose explosive effect, had it failed, would have been global: nuclear war was only one step away when the Americans discovered that the neighbouring island of Cuba was being equipped with Russian ballistic missiles. Kennedy managed to dissuade the Russians from their venture and pave the way for the test-ban agreement (August 1963), which was his contribution to the lessening of tension in international relations. In 1968 the Johnson administration and Khrushchev's successors concluded an agreement directed against the proliferation of nuclear weapons. Rejected by France and China, but subscribed to by Great Britain and West Germany, it set the course for the relaxation of tension in the new decade.

The transition to the 1970s was marked by the rejection of Britain's second Common Market application in 1967, the conclusion of the Kennedy Round in the same year, and the continuation of America's hopeless involvement in the Vietnam War. However, the same period also witnessed events which opened up fresh horizons for the 1970s. The deaths of Winston Churchill (1965), Dwight D. Eisenhower (1967) and Konrad Adenauer (1967), together with President de Gaulle's retirement (1969) and President Johnson's rejection of a further term (1968), seemed to set the seal on the initial post-war period. The floor was taken by a post-war generation for whom the world-war era had no reality in personal experience.

Another social and cultural climate prevailed, too. Significant in this respect were the Second Vatican Council (1962–65) and papal intervention in major political controversies, the latter signalized by the Pope's visits to UN headquarters and Geneva, and by the Soviet premier's audience with Pope Paul VI in 1967.

The testing of China's first atom bomb in 1967 was a warning rendered still more cogent by the news (in 1970) of successful experiments with long-range rockets. The outlook for the 1970s was characterized by President Nixon's restatement of America's mission: a renunciation of the role of world policeman (the Guam Doctrine), the announcement of further troop withdrawals from Vietnam, and a prospect of withdrawals from Germany as well. The Hague conference of the EEC countries declared its readiness to resume negotiations with Britain and the other EFTA members. Germany moved back into the centre of the international scene when the Federal Republic took the initiative in opening east-west negotiations of its own, both with its eastern neighbours and with Moscow.

We are thus on the verge of a new attempt to heal the breach between east and west opened up in 1947 and establish a new order in Europe. The novel post-war feature is that, instead of striving to resolve matters by force of arms, Germany is seeking a solution on the basis of EEC, NATO and the Four-Power Treaty. It is noteworthy that the Soviet Union and the Warsaw Pact countries are angling for a 'European security conference', and that the western powers are prepared to study the possibility of such a conference, but only if Canada and the United States are guaranteed the right to participate.

An 'Atlantic system' does exist, therefore, even in the absence of supra-national Atlantic authorities. There are even Soviet diplomats who toy with the idea of some day, and in some way, associating the eastern bloc with NATO. When he spoke of a Europe extending from the Atlantic to the Urals, General de Gaulle was speaking for an old Europe that no longer exists.

The idea of One World is possibly our most important bequest from the United States. The Americans have abandoned the notion of being the *one* world power in this *one* world. After experimenting with global condominium in uneasy partnership with Soviet Russia, they are now habituating themselves to the old pattern of multiple states or multiple regions. That implies a return to the balance of power, and to a mental approach which gives scope for close US-European co-operation.

THE ECONOMIC SUBSTRUCTURE OF TRANSATLANTIC CO-OPERATION

The real basis of the closer relations between the United States and Europe is the former's huge economic potential. The United States could offer Europe two things which were beyond the capacity of the Soviet Union to provide immediately after the end of the war: a flow of goods and credit, and, in the event of a military threat, the use of atomic weapons.

91 Except for the relative lack of traffic, this street scene (1969) of Moscow is not remarkably different from a similar scene in the United States.

Because the Russians after 1949 also commanded the secret of nuclear fission and its military applications and rapidly outpaced the Americans in rocketry during the ensuing decade, there arose the possibility of a Soviet-American compromise. The eventual outcome, as we have already seen, was the growth of a super-power system, which in turn promoted the formation of regional sub-systems to which the super-powers themselves belonged. This applied to Russia *vis-à-vis* China just as it still applies to the United States and Europe.

The Soviet storm-clouds that loomed over the first few post-war years emitted shafts of lightning which, as at an earlier date, sent thunder rolling across the capitalist world. Russia prophesied the downfall of the capitalist world, and the capitalist world feared a communist take-over in Western Europe. The target of Soviet economic planners was to overtake the west, America included, in prosperity and economic achievement. This proved to be a grand miscalculation. Only immense sacrifices in the consumer-goods sector enabled Soviet Russia to implement a programme which included the re-equipping of its armies with modern weapons, the creation of a nuclear arsenal, and the development of a first-class apparatus in the field of space technology.

By contrast, the United States managed to retain its lead not only in the civil and military sectors but also, ultimately, in space travel. The system of alliances built up by the United States includes – with

92 The United States buying up European scientists from slot machines labelled 'Physicists' and 'Chemists'; cartoon from *Krokodil*, 1969.

93, 94 US-Soviet competition in outer space: the astronauts Yuri Gagarin and Alan B. Shepard.

the exception of Russia – all the world's leading industrialized countries and the defeated powers of 1945. During the 1960s, Japan and Germany were only second to the super-powers in the economic league. The Soviet Union itself, although a major industrial power by virtue of its size and population, was able to play the part of a technological leader and distributor of know-how among its political friends only by the importation of capital goods and know-how – principally from its own satellites.

Not so the west. It should, of course, be recognized that the west also has adopted the concept of planning and the habit of thinking in planning categories. Running a war afforded the Allies experience of procedures which were developed further in the post-war period. As soon as the United States grasped that it could make its credit available to Europe during the immediate post-war crisis, and would thereby vastly strengthen its creditor position throughout the world, it 183 transformed a military commitment into one of an economic nature. In this way it perpetuated the system of Lend-Lease, originally devised in 1940, in another form. The very fact that World War II ended with success in nuclear fission and the building of the atom bomb positively dictated that programming and planning should continue in the future.

During the 1940s and 1950s the United States engaged in planning to a degree which surpassed all expectations. In providing military and economic aid, it not only transferred goods and funds, not only sent businessmen and experts all over the world, but also demonstrated the presence of US power by means of its soldiers and fighting units on land, on sea and in the air.

In war-time, co-operation between government and industry was taken for granted. The vast economic growth of the post-war period was founded on such co-operation. In some western countries – notably France – it took the form of state planning proper, but the influence of government on economic activity was immense, even where no state planning authorities were set up. The Truman Doctrine, the Marshall Plan, the Point Four programme, the Alliance for Progress, but, above all, nuclear fission and fusion, earth-satellites and lunar exploration – all these were state-sponsored projects which summoned a new era into being.

The position has been neatly stated by Professor M. M. Postan. Whereas economic progress had hitherto been regarded as an autonomous historical process, it was now realized that this process could be guided by means of premeditated action and planning. From now on, the future could be delivered by instalments and the historical process was turned upside down. Man 'lived' the future; the past was a 'quarry' which supplied building materials to be fitted together in the present with an eye to the future. The irreversibility of time assumed by the biological sciences was projected into cultural history. Thus, planning became a form of research, and one which in the United States was largely government-sponsored.

This view of the future conflicted with both the liberal and Marxist conceptions of the world; but it was based on the ideas which animated the age of enlightenment, the breeding-ground for all modern patterns of development. There was a patent convergence between west and east during this new era in so far as both shared the belief in technological progress. (Small wonder that the Soviet physicist

Andrei Sakharov complained in an open letter to his government that bureaucratic red-tape was preventing Russia from matching the advances made by the United States.)

At the same time a new social awareness made itself felt throughout the entire world. Everyone everywhere wished and was meant to participate in universal prosperity. The principles of full employment and care for the elderly were accepted as a matter of course. In Britain, the health service was taken over by the state, and other countries adopted indirect forms of state-regulated medicine. These claims upon the state resulted in state control of the economy through fiscal policy and government expenditure. And since military expenditure accounted for a substantial proportion of the budget, it was not incorrect to speak of a 'military-industrial complex'. While this 'growth economy' proved to be much more stable than the preceding 'free market economy', it possessed flaws of its own, particularly the phenomenon of excess demand, which held a risk of permanent inflation.

The United States' economic offensive – following upon the blunder of precipitate demobilization and disentanglement from obligations assumed during the war (1945–47) – was so formulated in the Marshall Plan as not to exclude the countries of Eastern Europe. The Soviet Union was unwilling to admit foreign experts, however. It cut itself off from economic co-operation with the United States, and so, at the Soviet Union's behest, did the other countries of the communist bloc, which, as a result, effectively became its satellites.

The initial period – the 'heroic' years from 1948 to 1953 – produced some admirable examples of transatlantic co-operation, both political and economic. This was when the whole outline of a new political conception took shape: the catastrophic legacy of the past was liquidated and the outcome was the first phase of European recovery.

The architects of the new era, Bevin and Monnet, Schuman, de Gasperi and Adenauer, working in harness with Paul Hoffman and the other OEEC experts, focused their efforts at reconstruction on the idea of an economically united Europe, while the British sought to renew the war-time alliance by means of the Brussels Five-Power Treaty (1948), and the Americans provided military aid for Europe through NATO.

The United States did not repeat the mistakes it had made over reparations in the 1920s. This time it footed part of the bill for Europe's reconstruction but stipulated, in return, that domestic inflation should be halted by devaluation, in other words, by alignment with the world market. From 1950 onwards the Korean War provided a massive stimulus to economic expansion.

The minor recession of 1953 was followed by four years of consolidation, flourishing growth and recovery, now that the new European institutions had begun to function. From 1958 onwards, with the end of the Payments Union and the return to convertibility, there began a period marked by a substantial easing of trade restrictions. Europe came into possession of gold and dollar reserves.

In 1963, a new situation took shape. This was the year in which the United States received a stand-by loan from the Monetary Fund, in which, in other words, Europe lent its support to the US Federal Reserve Bank. With the transformation in 1961 of the OEEC into the OECD, that is to say, of a European into a joint European, American and Canadian body, the way was paved for linking the new developments in Europe with those in the United States. The Americans, on their side, departed from their protectionist traditions by passing the Trade Expansion Act, and Kennedy inaugurated the moves which led to the GATT conferences of later years, at which a moderately protectionist United States was to sit at the negotiating table with a moderately protectionist Europe.

The United States thus volunteered to smooth the path to economic growth by liberalizing foreign trade. The scheme proved a success. Foreign trade grew proportionately faster than the gross national product. Europe and the United States escaped from a system of physical controls (quotas) and bilateralism, the EEC and EFTA declared war on commercial discrimination within their own regions, and GATT provided an instrument with which inter-regional adjustments could be made.

But in the middle and later years of the 1960s a new problem arose – that of the United States' adverse balance of payments. The year 1963 has been christened 'the end of the dollar era', i.e. the end of public loans by the US government, though they were succeeded by corporate investment. US investments in Europe were then running at 28–29 billion dollars. From 1962 onwards, the American trade balance no longer displayed the high surpluses of former years. This meant that increased demands from abroad could no longer be met by rising exports. The competitive position of the United States, which

186

95 The Hilton Hotel in Brussels, one visible form of US investment in Europe.

had already deteriorated once towards the end of the 1950s, had improved again when Europe entered a period of mounting inflation. After 1967, however, the United States also fell prey to an inflationary trend which far surpassed that of Europe.

This twofold phenomenon – balance of payments deficit and inflation, or worldwide indebtedness and the danger of spreading inflation because of mounting dollar reserves in Europe – impaired the standing and prestige of the United States. It damaged itself still further with its plan to 'plug' foreign indebtedness by means of statutory purchasing contracts linked with US firms, a policy which only boosted America's cost of living and undermined the value of the dollar from within. (H. Schelbert demonstrated in 1968 that 7 out of every 10 million dollars of foreign exchange savings are lost because of additional domestic costs.)

The upshot was that in 1968 large-scale speculation against the dollar began, and the price of gold rose to $44.36 as against the official rate of $35 per ounce. Although the adoption of a dual price system for gold succeeded in stabilizing the dollar's position as a world currency, discussion of currency revaluation now assumed practical significance. Europeans were only applying Kennedy's principle of 'participation' and Nixon's reversion to the balance of power to the question of the monetary system when they incorporated plans for a European monetary system in the agenda of the EEC.

The aim at the 1944 Bretton Woods conference – parallel in the economic sphere with Dumbarton Oaks, where plans for UNO were evolved – was to restore order in the world by setting up global economic institutions, e.g. the International Monetary Fund (IMF) and the International Bank for Reconstruction and Development (IBRD). Strangely enough, the IMF only came into operation when the gravest problems had already been overcome without its aid, and the IBRD would never have got off the ground at all if the US government had not launched its own much larger schemes. The United States promoted its trade liberalization policy in a highly effective way by giving preferential treatment to Europe and by co-operating vigorously within the organizations which owed their existence to the Marshall Plan. Having passed through a forty-year period (thirty-seven years, to be precise) characterized by a dollar gap, which was synonymous with a European deficit, the world entered a phase of European surplus, which amounts to a dollar deficit.

This was essentially the result of an economic recovery which lured US capital to Europe, particularly after the creation of the European Common Market made it attractive for enterprise to set up business behind its tariff walls. US capital growth (direct investments) in the field of industrial production increased at an annual rate of 21 per cent in the period 1958–65 as compared with 16·5 per cent in the period 1953–58.

The persistent and usually increasing deficit in America's balance of payments (3–4 billion dollars from 1958 onwards, declining later, but back again to 3 billions by 1967) – in other words, rising US indebtedness – resulted in an alarming outflow of gold (in 1949 amounting to 24·6 billion dollars; in 1968 to 10·5 billions). Short-term dollar debts, which had amounted to 8·2 billions in 1949, stood at 33 billion dollars in 1968.

Although external trade was on the increase and exports exceeded imports, total outgoings on capital account, foreign aid and other transactions far exceeded the surplus on the balance of trade. After 1957 the ratio of export surpluses to capital transfers deteriorated because external trade underwent no comparable increase, whereas military commitments, loans, government investments and private capital transfers all contributed to a flow of capital abroad. The competitive position of the United States steadied between 1960 and 1963, and the position remained good until 1967, because industrial costs in the United States were lower than in Western Europe, Italy excepted. Prices rose in all western countries from 1967 onwards, but the United States eventually overtook almost every European country in terms of rising inflation. Nixon, as Republican candidate in 1968, pledged himself to check this trend.

Those who harboured doubts about European recovery in the immediate post-war period were mistaken. They reckoned without America's contribution (as did the Americans themselves). The recovery of Europe and the expansion of the US economy went hand in hand. One token of this was the emergence of a Eurodollar market and the fact that the dollar became the chief reserve currency. France alone tried to change this situation by converting her dollar reserves into gold, but the disinclination of the central banks of other industrialized countries to follow the French lead, and their readiness to hold dollars as reserve funds showed that the desire to maintain co-operation with the United States was still strong. In relation to the 189 major problems of monetary policy, economic development and trade, the two areas had drawn much closer together, in that everyone accepted the principle of free trade and the liberalization of the money and capital markets as a guide-line. There was at least an approximation to the notion of a worldwide economic system, though indirectly, by way of regional 'blocs', customs unions, the Common Market, etc. All these promoted internal free trade in the regions concerned and came together at a higher, 'inter-bloc', level (the Kennedy Round) in an attempt to approach a general integration of markets through reciprocal concessions.

Within the EEC, US business ventures proved to be the strongest integrating factor, because in a number of countries – and in important sectors of industrial production – they commanded the greatest financial backing.

The immense success of Jean-Jacques Servan-Schreiber's book, *The American Challenge*, is not only symptomatic but is itself evidence of the phenomenon of far-reaching and reciprocal US-European interaction. How otherwise could one speak of a 'challenge', and how otherwise would it have been possible to suggest that the answer to it was for Europe to follow in America's footsteps? Since the appearance of Servan-Schreiber's book in 1968 the Americans have been experiencing a 'European challenge', to the extent that Europe's monetary position has improved just as America's has deteriorated. Significantly, European investments in the United States are latterly showing a greater percentage increase than US investments in Europe. What is dramatic about the situation is the fact that the crisis of confidence represents a threat to America's position in foreign affairs as much as it does to its economic leadership. The immense financial burden generated by the Vietnam War threatens to make the balance of payments deficit a permanent feature. Nixon's Guam Doctrine and his promise to withdraw American ground troops from Vietnam were a hint that, in reviewing its foreign policy commitments, the United States likewise proposed to review its external – and extreme – economic overcommitment.

96 European investment in the United States: The Pan Am Building in the heart of New York City represents a British participation, via the Cotton-Clore City Centre Properties group, of £9 million in a total investment of £36 million.

Under American influence, Europe has entered upon a new era. Europe's position in the world could never have undergone so fundamental a change had it not been for the United States. Europeans of the nineteenth century made it their aim to refashion the world in the spirit of Europe and furnish it with European goods and values. Their aim is far closer to fulfilment today, but things have not come about in the way they foresaw. The creation of rival colonial empires, which seemed to offer Germany a chance of establishing itself as the dominant European power and gaining a colonial empire as well, ended in the greatest political and social crisis of modern times, and gave Russia and the United States, the two great flanking powers, an opportunity to wield more influence over international developments than even they could have hoped for.

The idea of overseas colonial empires was rejected by the United States and Russia; they had evolved their own methods of colonization, in the form of a continuing stream of settlers and a steadily advancing frontier. By supporting independence movements in colonial territories, the United States made a breach in the old world order.

The emancipation of colonial peoples was the major development of the period which succeeded World War II. Soviet Russia facilitated Mao Tse-tung's accession, and thus spread the communist net across the whole of Northern and Central Asia. The United States released the Philippines from their colonial relationship and encouraged Indonesia's transition to independence. It was a trend, accepted by the British, which led by way of India to the dismantling of the whole structure of the Empire and the Commonwealth, and which gave rise to a movement of emancipation culminating, particularly in Africa, in the emergence of a long series of new countries. The same process was encouraged by France once her attempt to retain the French colonial empire had proved abortive. Thus occurred the transition from the age of imperialism and the balance of power to the   193

97 A soldier on guard in Washington, D.C., at the time of a riot following the murder of Dr Martin Luther King in April 1968.

age of the super-powers, dominated by Soviet Russia and the United States.

The roots of the process lay in the ceaseless change in the conditions of human life and human society. The Soviet Union and the United States had both made trail-blazing advances in the invention and application of new technological processes during the inter-war years. The Soviet Union was going over to economic planning at the time of the Great Depression; in America, the 1920s represented the beginning of a second industrial revolution. After the crisis provoked by the Great Depression, the United States proceeded through the New Deal and participation in World War II to build up an economic system which had little in common with the one that had existed previously.

War-time co-operation among the Allies was to be developed into a worldwide system of economic expansion by means of an international monetary fund, a bank for reconstruction and development, and an agency for the regulation of foreign trade, additional instruments being the Marshall Plan, foreign aid and development aid. Soviet Russia became a model and example to large parts of Asia and Africa, and also a training centre for aspirants to a new, state-controlled system of public welfare; in the west, the United States became the leading economic power, often a mentor and example to budding technologists but always – partly in competition with Russia – a purveyor of investment capital and consumer goods.

The combination of rapid technological and industrial development and radical changes in the international political system endows the present era with the characteristics of a revolutionary epoch. We live in a climate of international tension. The threat of war has been our constant companion. Although 'World War III' has not broken out, the post-war period was characterized by revolutions (China, Cuba), insurrections (East Germany, Poland, Hungary, Czechoslovakia), changes of régime (Egypt, Iraq, etc.), a series of colonial liquidations, and protracted local wars (Korea, Indo-China, Algeria, Israel, Vietnam, the Congo, Nigeria, India).

The term 'military-industrial complex' has been coined to cover a characteristic feature of our age, of which the military-industrial system is indeed a part. Once again it was the United States that became the leader and example in this respect, and once again it did so in competition with Soviet Russia. The United States' trans-

formation from a bourgeois state *par excellence* into a military, technological and industrial society is a clear indication of the basic changes
in the western world. The country which in 1940 was the 'arsenal of
democracy' has become the seat of western military planning and
leadership; it has also remained an arsenal.

The most notable development in the relations of the United States
and Europe, and one which possesses symbolic significance because
it represents a watershed in world history, was the manufacture of the
atom bomb. Scientists and technologists on both sides in World War
II competed fiercely in developing this weapon of mass destruction,
aware that the winner of the race would win the war. The United
States got there first. Two bombs dropped by US aircraft over
Hiroshima and Nagasaki brought about the immediate end of the
war with Japan and, thus, of World War II itself. Military experts
had reckoned on a further duration of two years.

The manufacture of the atom bomb not only has a place in the
history of war, science and technology, as one might expect, but is
closely tied up with the whole political and intellectual history of the
twentieth century. The initial suggestion of the potentially decisive
importance of the project came from men who had been welcomed
by the United States after Hitler had expelled them on racial and
political grounds. Albert Einstein inspired a memorandum drafted by
two physicists (but signed by himself) which was personally handed
to President Roosevelt on 11 October 1939. It drew attention to the
experiments in nuclear fission then being conducted in a number of
countries and pointed out that, if applied in practice, the principle of
nuclear fission might produce a militarily decisive weapon. On
6 December 1941, one day before Pearl Harbor, President Roosevelt
approved a proposal from a committee of experts that plans for
making an atom bomb should go ahead. The 'District Manhattan'
project was subordinated to the War Department and entrusted to the
military. Thousands of scientists were engaged on it. Great Britain
sent its own scientists and further collaboration was later approved by
Roosevelt and Churchill.

The problem of the atom and hydrogen bomb still overshadows
the entire field of military and political activity. The Russians succeeded in exploding an A-bomb in 1949 and an H-bomb in 1953. In
1957 they sent the first earth-satellite, Sputnik I, into orbit round the
earth. This achievement, a product of the Russians' lead in rocketry 195

98, 99, 100, 101, 102, 103 The international impact of space exploration as shown on postage stamps from Cuba, Bulgaria, Czechoslovakia, Rumania, the Mongolian Republic and the United States.

techniques, came as a hard blow to the United States and gravely damaged its prestige in Europe. However, the Americans not only recovered, but took 'Sputnik' as a signal for self-examination, particularly in regard to their educational system and the training of scientists and technicians. Once again the United States profited from the collaboration of German experts (e.g. Wernher von Braun), who had preferred to go overseas after the war rather than remain in the Old World and who thus contributed to transatlantic integration. When John F. Kennedy called upon his fellow countrymen to solve the problem of a lunar landing within the next ten years, they succeeded before the ten years' period was finished and before the Russians could forestall them.

The effect of the military-industrial system, backed by nuclear energy, has been to facilitate Russian and American development of super-power status and to introduce a state of global peace based on a 'balance of terror'. America's political relations with Europe have suffered in the process, and the same applies to Soviet Russia's relations with its allies. The initial American nuclear monopoly, although it soon became no more than a temporary lead, was the reason for that 'asymmetrical' system of alliance known as NATO.

Any general assessment of the relationship between the United States and Europe must give prominence to the trends which have conduced to the present situation. The characteristic feature of that situation is that neither the United States nor the Soviet Union feels entirely comfortable about its quasi-monopoly, and that both super-powers are being moved to re-examine their relationship with their allies.

We can distinguish three phases in the process by which this came about. In the first, close US-British co-operation led to a trans-formation of the Western European union into the North Atlantic military alliance, to which the new German Federal Republic was eventually admitted. Economically buttressed by the Marshall Plan and militarily shielded by NATO, new forces arose in Europe which sought to realize the objective which had been assigned to Europe by the United States: the formation of a European union.

The second phase saw France, grown more self-confident under General de Gaulle's leadership, resist the development of a new Europe under Anglo-Saxon aegis (although this was what Clemenceau him-self had hoped for in 1919). By claiming a third seat at the Anglo-American boardroom table, de Gaulle conveyed the message that France was one of the victorious powers and that, if the western powers failed to grasp that message, France would seek and secure a hearing from Soviet Russia. He countered the Anglo-American special relationship with one between France and Russia.

During the third phase, the situation has been clarified to the extent that both Russia and the United States have brought developments which they have initiated to a logical conclusion. US encouragement of the EEC has set Britain on the road to union with continental Europe, and the Soviet Union has entered into negotiations with the German Federal Republic with a view to stabilizing Central Europe and gaining international recognition for the German Democratic Republic. This, by 1971, had virtually been achieved.

The attempt – supported by Great Britain during the 1950s – to convert Central Europe into a power-political vacuum has failed. The new Europe depends militarily on co-operation between an 197

American supreme command and German troops who hold the West German border in company with US units. The Anglo-American and Franco-Russian special relationships have thus lost much of their original value.

Both the tensions of the post-war period and the swift tempo of development which marked it were the result of fundamental shifts and cross-currents in the positions of the leading powers. The divergence between Marxism and capitalism is being countered by a trend towards convergence which stems – as we have shown – from the common American and Soviet problem of the military-industrial establishment and the universally accepted principle of co-operation between government and industry.

Misunderstandings, recriminations, intrigues and propaganda were an inevitable result of decolonization and the liquidation of the European empires, since the whole process was inextricably involved in the confrontation between the United States and the Soviet Union. The European powers were, in fact, living up to the very slogan that had been broadcast to the world at large by the Americans and Russians: freedom for the colonial peoples! But owing to the political circumstances in which it was carried out, this 'liberation' was seized upon by the Russians and Americans alike as an opportunity to carry their struggle into the Third World and pursue it there under the banner of aid. With the single exception of Germany, all the storm-centres of the post-war period – Korea, Laos, Vietnam, the Near East, the Congo, Cuba, India – have grown out of a post-colonial situation.

The Suez crisis of 1956 reflected the whole muddle and confusion of the post-war situation. The western powers made a final attempt to retrieve something of their former position as colonial powers. The Americans held aloof for the very reason that they declined to be labelled colonialists, and the Russians took advantage of disarray in the western camp to play the part of benevolent guardian in the Near East and simultaneously to mask the true nature of their intervention in Hungary.

In the current conflict in the Middle East the Suez crisis continues to smoulder. In a reversal of fronts, the countries of Western Europe, and in particular France, have taken revenge on America and have swung towards Egypt. For its part, the United States is trying, under cover of its pro-Israel policy, to retain and reinforce its position in the Mediterranean.

The very fact that the Americans and Russians turned the struggle for the Third World in this way into an east–west confrontation gave Europe an opportunity to adopt the position of a 'third force'. The situation in the west was clarified after the Suez affair, at least to the extent that Europe managed to surmount the second Berlin crisis. Instead the Vietnam War took the central position. Although there still seemed a possibility in Kennedy's day that it might be terminated in the same way as the Korean War, the situation grew worse under President Johnson.

By 1970 the west had reached a turning-point. The initial post-war period was over, and the question now was to map out the lines of policy on the basis of a new power structure.

Although there has been criticism of its structure and relevance, the North Atlantic alliance still forms the military and political basis of the western position. Responsibilities are shared between the United States and Europe, the former providing the nuclear shield while the latter makes a substantial contribution in terms of conventional weapons. As long as the United States remains in Central Europe with a strong military force of its own, it renders the alliance credible as a political system.

Moves towards independence noticeable in the western and eastern camps alike, China's ideological conflict with the Soviet Union and the EEC's attempts to strengthen Europe by means of supra-national institutions mean that the super-powers owe their super-status to nuclear armaments alone. And yet the development of these and other weapons not only imposes an enormous economic burden on both countries, but has become largely pointless in view of the relaxation of tension between eastern and western blocs. Hence Americans increasingly speak of a transition to a new balance of power. This they envisage as a system of 'regions': America, Western Europe, the Soviet Union, and Japan (China). These industrial regions, which are all situated in the northern hemisphere, would have a common goal, namely, to assist the developing countries in the southern hemisphere.

If present trends are any indication, they suggest that Europe may advance more quickly than the United States in the creation of supra-national institutions on a regional European basis. The America which, first through the League of Nations and then through UNO, the IMF, the International Bank and the Marshall Plan agencies, gave the original impetus to the formation of supra-national authorities, in 199 short the America which championed the idea of One World, found itself in the throes of a deep-seated crisis at the beginning of the 1970s. Reverses in Asia, beginning with the 'loss' of China and followed by the Korean stalemate and the interminable Vietnam War, shook America's confidence in its claim to be the leader of the free world. Nixon's success in the 1968 election represented a yearning for the good old days – in other words, for disengagement and neo-isolationism.

In 1971 events altered rapidly. It soon became evident that the assumptions of the previous two or three decades had now lost at least some of their value and usefulness. New developments in the world economy which came to a head in the final years of the 1960s meant that the ground rules of Europe's relationship with America, and America's with Europe, had to be worked out once more.

A crisis of America's own making broke out on 15 August 1971 when President Nixon suspended conversion of the dollar into gold by means of an embargo on the export of gold, imposed a ten per cent surcharge on imports into America, and announced a reduction in the foreign aid programme as well as in the US budget.

104 The familiar American tourist in Europe since the mid-1960s has been the student or the hippy carrying the minimum of belongings. In the summer of 1970 the young tourists shown here were stranded and sought, in front of the American Express office in London, to sell whatever they could.

105 President Pompidou and President Nixon during the conference that took place in the Azores in December 1971 as a result of the international money crisis. After this meeting the United States announced the virtual devaluation of the dollar.

This time – unlike the economic crisis of 1929–32 – the crisis was not provoked by an internal breakdown in the American economy, but by a failure of financial policy, brought about by the collapse of the United States' international credit position. The role of the dollar as a gold and reserve currency was made impossible by a balance of payments deficit of eleven billion dollars, and by the new phenomenon of a deficit in the balance of trade (where traditionally a surplus had been shown). In view of short-term foreign indebtedness amounting in summer 1971 to 57·4 billion dollars and diminishing gold reserves of no more than ten billion dollars the situation was catastrophic. The president did more than note this dangerous situation; he initiated an entirely new economic, financial and trading policy, and required that America's trade partners should seek for new solutions 201 too. In so doing he provoked a confrontation among America and its economic allies, in particular Western Europe.

For the first time in the course of transatlantic relations America and Europe are meeting each other on equal terms. Nixon's appeal to the ties of community and interest between both sides of the Atlantic is reminiscent of the pleas of European statesmen, menaced by the prospect of World War II, that America should renounce its isolationist stance. Nixon's 'new era' is taking shape; the central importance of transatlantic relations is increasingly obvious. It would be disastrous if Europe and America were now, as they did in the 1930s, to retreat into an obstinate seclusion – those who cry 'America First' into a 'Fortress America', the Europeans into a separatist EEC.

Recognizing Europe's historic mission, President Nixon has placed his European policy in a central position, while at the same time withdrawing America's claims to hegemony and taking the initial steps towards settling the mutual positions of the Atlantic partners; he has thus created a balance of power between the two continents. President Monroe disentangled America from Europe; as a superpower, America wanted after World War II to make Europe a first line of defence against its chief rival; now America intends to work with a stronger Europe towards reconciliation with Russia. Indeed, America has the opportunity to win a measure of influence over Russia by means of its policy towards China, for Russia will remain America's greatest rival as long as Europe remains disunited.

In the 1950s and 1960s, Europe felt the pressure of American economic power; it is now America's turn to fear the same power, this time wielded by Europe. But the current crisis involves far more than mere economic supremacy. America and Europe now have to face their responsiblity for the post-industrial era, on which we have now embarked, and to turn their attention to the problems of the Third World. That world will supply us with criteria by which we can give a deeper meaning to our own civilization.

The foregoing survey has carried us through a singular sequence of events. As one arrives at the end, the impression is that Europe is moving towards an American pattern, while America has acquired the complex and confusing role of an imperial power in the Victorian mould. In aligning itself with the American form of industrial establishment Europe is assimilating America's achievements only

106, 107 The Stoa of Attalos in the Agora of Athens: a reconstruction paid for by American funds. Below, London Bridge, bought by American entrepreneurs, was re-erected near Havasu City, Arizona, in October 1971.

to set up in competition with America, in order to preserve its former position of leadership. In turning to European forms of imperial power, America risks losing sight of its mission and breaking links with a Europe far removed from that of the heyday of imperialism.

The United States and Europe have drawn closer in the course of two centuries of history, but they have also drawn apart. Each has taught the other in turn. They can have but one common goal and ideal: to be a light to lighten themselves and the One World, of which they are both a part.

SELECTED READING

In view of the scope of my subject, which has been directly or indirectly discussed by thousands of writers, only a selective list of relevant publications can be quoted here. As well as books which have been used in the present study, the reader's attention is drawn to others whose approach to the subject differs from mine.

My selection includes not only literature immediately available in Zurich but also monographs I consulted elsewhere in Europe and in the United States. Works by American authors predominate because America, or the United States, constitutes my real theme. There are also works by British, German-speaking and French writers – and some others besides – who have made important contributions to the American theme and may be said to speak for Europe.

It seemed most useful to classify my bibliography under the following headings: I *Confrontation* (works which specifically set out to compare the United States with Europe); II *Historical Perspectives* (works affording a general view of trends in US development); III *Aspects of American Culture* (works which, although not aimed at comparison, are consciously or unconsciously written from the 'European angle'); and, the main category, IV *Transatlantic Relations* (comprising general accounts and specialized works on foreign policy).

I have on principle confined myself almost entirely to works published since World War II and have refrained from listing memoirs and political biographies for reasons of space.

I CONFRONTATION

Allen, H.C. and Hill, C.P. (edd.) *British Essays in American History*. London 1957

Barraclough, Geoffrey 'Europa, Amerika und Russland in Vorstellung und Denken des 19. Jahrhunderts'. In *Historische Zeitschrift* 1966

Baudry, Bernard *Euro-America*. Paris 1962

Cartier, Raymond *L'Europe à la Conquête de l'Amérique*. Paris 1956

Commager, Henry Steele *America in Perspective: The United States through Foreign Eyes*. New York 1947

Der Monat vol. 5, no. 50 (November 1952) 'Europa und Amerika (ein dokumentarischer Streifzug von E. Franzen und M.J. Lasky)', from which a number of quotations on pages 15 and 17 are taken

Fabian, Bernhard *Alexis de Tocquevilles Amerikabild*. Heidelberg 1957

Fraenkel, Ernst *Amerika im Spiegel des deutschen politischen Denkens*. Cologne 1959

Herm, Gerhard *Amerika erobert Europa*. Düsseldorf 1964

Hölzle, Erwin *Geschichte der zweigeteilten Welt (Amerika und Russland)*. Hamburg 1961

Koht, Halvdan *The American Spirit in Europe*. Philadelphia 1949, from which the quotations on page 23 are taken

Mandel, Ernest *Europe versus America? Contradictions of Imperialism.* London 1970

Mann, Golo *Geschichte und Geschichten.* Frankfurt 1961

Mousset, Paul *Essai sur l'Américain Moyen.* Paris 1958

Pelling, Henry *America and the British Left. From Bright to Bevan.* New York 1957

Penrose, E. T. *The Revolution in International Relations: a study in the Changing Balance of Power.* London 1965

Proudfoot, M. J. *European Refugees 1939–1952: a Study in Forced Population Movement.* London 1957

Servan-Schreiber, Jean-Jacques *The American Challenge.* London 1968

Skard, Sigmund *The American Myth and the European Mind.* Philadelphia 1961

Sommer, Walter *Die Weltmacht USA im Urteil der Französischen Publizistik 1924–1939.* Tübingen 1967

Toynbee, Arnold J. *America and the World Revolution.* London 1962

Urzidil, Johannes *Das Glück der Gegenwart (Goethes Amerikabild).* Zurich 1958

Westin, Alan F. (ed.) *Views of America.* New York 1966

Williams, Francis *The American Invasion.* London 1962

II HISTORICAL PERSPECTIVES

Allen, F. L. *The Big Change: America transforms itself 1900–1950.* New York 1952

van Alstyne, R. W. *The Rising American Empire.* Oxford 1960

——*The Genesis of American Nationalism.* 1970

Ball, George *The Discipline of Power.* Boston 1968

Barraclough, Geoffrey *An Introduction to Contemporary History.* London 1966

Boorstin, Daniel *America and the Image of Europe.* New York 1960

Cochran, Thomas *The American Business System.* Cambridge, Mass. 1957

Curti, Merle *Probing our Past.* New York 1955

——*American Philanthropy Abroad: A History.* New York 1963

Cushing, Strout *The American Image of the Old World.* New York 1963

Fleming, D. and Bailyn, B. *Perspectives in American History.* Vol. I (pp. 123–286) Ernest R. May *American Imperialism: A Reinterpretation.* Cambridge, Mass. 1967. Vol. II *The Intellectual Migration: Europe and America 1930–1960.* Cambridge, Mass. 1968

Handlin, Oscar *The Uprooted. (From the Old World to the New).* Boston 1951

Kohn, Hans *American Nationalism. An Interpretative Essay.* New York 1961

Langer, William L. *Explorations in Crisis. Papers on International History.* Cambridge, Mass. 1969

Laserson, M. M. *The American Impact on Russia, diplomatic and ideological, 1784–1907.* New York 1950

Lathan, Earl (ed.) *The Philosophy and Policies of Woodrow Wilson.* Chicago 1958

Lerner, Max *America as a Civilization: Life and Thought in the United States today.* New York 1957

Mayer, Arno J. *Political Origins of the New Diplomacy, 1917–1918.* New York 1959; new edition 1969

Mead, Robert O. *The Atlantic Legacy. Essays in American-European Cultural History.* New York 1968

Perkins, Dexter *The American Way (1787–1956).* Ithaca, N.Y. 1957

——*A History of the Monroe Doctrine.* Boston 1963

Pierson, G. W. *Tocqueville and Beaumont in America.* New York 1938

Sorenson, Thomas C. *The Story of American Propaganda.* New York 1968

Van Tassel, David D. and McAhren, R. W. (edd.) *European Origins of American Thought.* Chicago 1969

Vann Woodward, C. (ed.) *A Comparative Approach to American History (Forum Lectures).* Washington D.C. 1968

III ASPECTS OF AMERICAN CULTURE

Beloff, Max *The Great Powers: Essays in Twentieth-Century Politics.* London 1959

Borch, Herbert von *Die unfertige Gesellschaft.* Munich 1960

Brock, W. R. *The Character of American History.* London 1965

Brogan, Denis W. *America in the Modern World.* London 1960

——*American Aspects.* London 1964

Bruckberger, Raymond L. *The Image of America.* London 1960

Gorer, Geoffrey *The Americans.* New York 1948

Guggisberg, H. R. *Das europäische Mittelalter im amerikanischen Geschichtsdenken des 19. und 20. Jahrhunderts.* Basle 1964

den Hollander, A. N. J. and Skard, Sigmund (edd.) *American Civilization. An Introduction.* London 1969

Link, F. H. *Amerika – Vision und Wirklichkeit.* Frankfurt 1968

Lipson, E. *Reflections on Britain and the United States.* London 1959

McCloskey, R. G. *American Conservatism in the Age of Enterprise.* London 1964

Mann, Golo *Vom Geist Amerikas.* Zurich 1954

Nettles, C. P. *The Roots of American Civilization.* London 1964

Piovene, Guido *De America.* Milan 1954

Rappard, William E. *Die Ursachen der wirtschaftlichen Überlegenheit der Vereinigten Staaten.* Bern 1956

Schachtshabel, Hans G. *Automation in Wirtschaft und Gesellschaft.* Hamburg 1961

Schwarz, Urs *Strategie – gestern – heute – morgen. Die Entwicklung des politisch-militärischen Denkens in Amerika.* Düsseldorf 1965

Siegfried, André *America at Mid-Century.* London 1955

Stratowa, Wulf (ed.) *Spektrum Amerika – aus Werken 141 europäischer Dichter und Denker.* Vienna 1964

Thistlethwaite, Frank *The Great Experiment. An Introduction to the History of the American People.* Cambridge 1961

Watt, D. G. *Personalities and Policies.* London 1965

IV TRANSATLANTIC RELATIONS

US FOREIGN POLICY SINCE 1900

Adler, Selig *The Uncertain Giant, 1921–1941. American Foreign Policy between the Wars.* New York 1965

Bohlen, C. E. *The Transformation of American Foreign Policy.* New York 1970

Carleton, William G. *The Revolution in American Foreign Policy: its Global Range.* New York 1963

Duroselle, J. B. *From Wilson to Roosevelt. Foreign Policy of the United States 1913–1945.* Cambridge, Mass. 1963

Grenville, J. A. S. 'Diplomacy and War Plans in the United States, 1890–1917'. In *Transactions of the Royal Historical Society* 1961

Halle, Louis *The Cold War as History.* London 1967

Horowitz, David *From Yalta to Vietnam: American Foreign Policy in the Cold War.* 4th ed., Harmondsworth 1969

Kennan, George *American Diplomacy, 1900–1950.* Chicago 1951

Lafeber, Walter *America, Russia and the Cold War, 1945–1966.* New York 1967

Leopold, Richard W. *The Growth of American Foreign Policy.* New York 1962 and 1967

Osgood, R., Tucker, R. W. *et al.* (edd.) *America and the World. From the Truman Doctrine to Vietnam.* Baltimore and London 1970

Spanier, John W. *American Foreign Policy since World War II.* 3rd rev. ed., London 1970

Westerfield, H. Bradford *The Instruments of American Foreign Policy.* New York 1963

PROBLEMS OF ATLANTIC RELATIONS AND EUROPEAN INTEGRATION

Adler, Selig *The Isolationist Impulse. Its twentieth century reaction.* New York 1957

Allen, H. C. *The Anglo-American Predicament: the British Commonwealth, the United States, and European Unity.* London 1960

Alting von Geusau, Frans A. M. *Beyond the European Community.* Leyden 1969

Barraclough, Geoffrey *European Unity in Thought and Action.* Oxford 1963

Bell, Coral *The Debatable Alliance. An Essay in Anglo-American Relations.* Oxford 1964

Beloff, Max *The United States and the Unity of Europe.* London 1963

Bourne, Kenneth *Britain and the Balance of Power in North America, 1815–1908.* London 1967

Cleveland, Harold van B. *The Atlantic Idea and its European Rivals.* New York and London 1966

Dehio, Ludwig *Germany and World Politics in the Twentieth Century.* London 1959

Deutsch, Karl *et al. France, Germany and the Western Alliance.* New York 1967

Freymond, Jacques *Die Atlantische Welt.* In Golo Mann (ed.) *Die Welt von Heute.* Berlin 1961

——*Western Europe since the War. A short political history.* New York and London 1964

Kissinger, Henry A. *The Troubled Partnership. A Reappraisal of the Atlantic Alliance.* New York 1965

Pfaltzgraff, Robert L. (Jr) *The Atlantic Community. A Complex Imbalance.* New York and London 1969

Seton-Watson, Hugh *Neither War, nor Peace: the Struggle for Power in the Post-War World.* London 1960

Urwin, Derek W. *Western Europe since 1945. A Short Political History.* London 1968

ECONOMIC ASPECTS

Baldwin, David A. *Economic Development and American Foreign Policy, 1943–1962.* Chicago and London 1966

Ellsworth, P. T. *The International Economy.* 4th ed., Toronto 1969

Gardner, Lloyd C. *Economic Aspects of New Deal Diplomacy.* Madison 1964

Hellmann, Rainer *Amerika auf dem Europa-Markt. US-Direkt-Investitionen im Gemeinsamen Markt.* Baden-Baden 1966
——*Weltunternehmen nur amerikanisch? Das Ungleichgewicht der Investitionen zwischen Amerika und Europa.* Baden-Baden 1970
Schelbert-Syfrig, Heidi *Das 'Buy-American'-Prinzip und die amerikanische Zahlungsbilanz.* Zurich 1968
Thomas, Brinley *Migration and Economic Growth: a study of Great Britain and the Atlantic Economy.* Cambridge 1954

POLITICAL RELATIONS WITH INDIVIDUAL COUNTRIES

France
Blumenthal, Henry *France and the United States. Their Diplomatic Relations, 1789–1914.* Chapel Hill 1970

Germany
Berg, Peter *Deutschland und Amerika 1918–1929.* Lübeck and Hamburg 1963
Jäckle, Ernst *Amerika und wir, 1926–1951: amerikanisch-deutsches Ideenbündnis.* Stuttgart 1951
Moltmann, Günter *Amerikas Deutschlandpolitik im Zweiten Weltkrieg.* Heidelberg 1958
Offner, Arnold A. *American Appeasement. United States Foreign Policy and Germany, 1933–1938.* Cambridge, Mass. 1969

Great Britain
Allen, H. C. *The Anglo-American Relationship since 1783.* London 1959
Nicholas, H. C. *Britain and the United States.* London 1963
Russett, Bruce M. *Community and Contention. Britain and America in the 20th Century.* Cambridge, Mass. 1963

Netherlands
Vlekke, B. H. M. *The Netherlands and the United States.* Boston 1945

The Mediterranean Countries and Italy
Field, James A. (Jr) *America and the Mediterranean World, 1776–1882.* Princeton 1969
Hughes, H. Stuart *The United States and Italy.* Cambridge, Mass. 1953

Russia
Bailey, Thomas A. *America faces Russia. Russian-American Relations from Early Times to Our Day.* Gloucester 1964
Williams, William Appleman *American-Russian Relations 1781–1947.* New York 1952

Scandinavia
Scott, F. D. *The United States and Scandinavia.* Cambridge 1950

Switzerland
Meier, Heinz *Friendship under Stress. U.S.-Swiss Relations 1900–1950.* Bern 1970

Finland
Paasivirta, Jukani *The Victors in World War I and Finland.* Helsinki 1952

China
Fairbanks, John *The United States and China.* New York 1962

Ireland
Ward, Alan J. *Ireland and Anglo-American Relations 1899–1921.* London 1969

For further literature, particularly on literary and cultural relations, see Sigmund Skard, American Studies in Europe. *2 vols., Philadelphia 1958.*

LIST OF ILLUSTRATIONS

Interior, National Park Service, Edison National Historic Site

24 *Washington, La Fayette and Tench Tilghman at Yorktown*, painting by Charles Willson Peale, 1784; Maryland State House, Annapolis, Maryland

25 Design for Monticello, by Thomas Jefferson, from *Thomas Jefferson, Architect*, 1968. Photo RIBA

26 United States section at the Great Exhibition, 1851, lithograph from Dickinson's *Pictures of the Great Exhibition*; British Museum

27 Daniel Boone escorting settlers through the Cumberland Gap, painting by George Caleb Bingham, 1851–52; Washington University Gallery of Art, St Louis, Missouri

28 General Scott's entrance into Mexico City, 1847, lithograph by Bayot after C. Nebel, from *The War between the United States and America.*

29 *There Shall be no more War*, painting by J.O.J. Frost; Collection Nina Fletcher Little, Brookline, Mass.

30 *Battle of Hampton Roads*, 1862, lithograph; National Maritime Museum, Greenwich

31 Immigrant ship, 1850, engraving; Mansell Collection

32 Poster promoting settlements in South Dakota, lithograph by the Forbes Lith. Manufacturing Co., 1890; Prints and Photographs Division, Library of Congress, Washington, D.C.

33 Pioneer homestead with sod house in southeast Custer County, Nebraska, *c.* 1887; S.D. Butcher Collection, Nebraska Historical Society

34 Scene from the film *Shalako*, 1968. Photo Camera Press, Cesar Lucas

35 *The Rocky Mountains*, detail of painting by Albert Bierstadt, 1863; Metropolitan Museum of Art, Rogers Fund

36 *Square in Charleston*, painting by C.J. Hamilton, 1872; courtesy Abby Aldrich Rockefeller Folk Art Collection, Williamsburg, Virginia

37 'The Clipper of the Clouds in the Rocky Mountains', illustration by Benett for *Robur le Conquérant* by Jules Verne, 1886; British Museum

38 Charles Dickens in America, cartoon from the *Daily Joker*, 1867; British Museum

39 Oscar Wilde in America, cartoon by Thomas Nast from *Harper's Weekly*, June 1882; British Museum

40 *The Raven*, lithograph by Édouard Manet, 1875, illustration for E.A. Poe's poem, translated by Stéphane Mallarmé; British Museum

41 Henry James, detail of portrait by John Singer Sargent, 1913; National Portrait Gallery, London

42 Thomas Carlyle, painting by J.A.McN. Whistler, 1873; Glasgow Art Gallery

43 *Mrs William Page in Rome*, painting by William Page, 1860; Detroit Institute of Arts

44 Rear Admiral Sampson on the bridge of the *New York*, *Harper's Weekly*, May 1898; British Museum

45 Commodore Perry meeting Imperial Commission, 1854, engraving; Mansell Collection

46 American Methodist compound in China, from the *Graphic*, November 1893; Radio Times Hulton Picture Library

47 'The Big Thing', cartoon by Thomas Nast, from *Harper's Weekly*, May 1867; British Museum

48 The port of Hyogo, with the British and American fleets at anchor, 1868, engraving; Mansell Collection

49 Building the Panama Canal, 1910. Photo Organization of American States, Washington, D.C.

INDEX

Page numbers in italics refer to illustrations

216